fuchsia
a care manual

David Clark

LAUREL GLEN PUBLISHING

Publishing Director
Laura Bamford
Executive Editor
Julian Brown
Assistant Editor
Karen O'Grady
Executive Art Editor
Mark Winwood
Art Director
Keith Martin
Photography
Peter Myers
and Michael Gomez
Production Controller
Melanie Frantz
Picture Researcher
Liz Fowler

First published
in the United States by
Laurel Glen Publishing
5880 Oberlin Avenue, Suite 400
San Diego, CA 92121-9653
1-800-284-3580

Library of Congress
Cataloging-in-Publication Data
available on request.

Produced by Mandarin Offset
Printed in China

ISBN 1-57145-608-2

1 2 3 4 5 97 98 99 00 01

Contents

Introduction

Although my name is on the cover of this book, I feel guilty in claiming it as mine. It has been writing itself ever since I started growing fuchsias some 30 years ago. Although this book contains much of the knowledge I have acquired over this period, it is inevitably a distillation of the combined experiences of my own with that of many other fuchsia growers. For the first 16 years of my working life I was employed in a large research institute engaged in preparing new horticultural, medical, and cosmetics products. My contributions to fuchsia growing are more related to the science of the subject than to that of the mysterious black art that sometimes seems to surround it.

I know of the problems that worry many growers by meeting them at various events such as the Chelsea Flower Show and at my nurseries. I have also learned that not all of these problems have been answered in the previous four books I have written on fuchsias. I hope that many of these deficiencies have now been addressed and rectified in this new work.

Fuchsia cultivation has changed very little in the last half-century and in some ways progress has been halted or reversed. No longer can we afford the time to grow the marvellous specimens that were seen at flower shows at the start of the 20th century. However, we have many new and wonderful cultivars that would have delighted the early growers and our understanding of plant nutrition has increased immensely since those days.

World-wide there are hundreds of new fuchsia cultivars introduced every year. Very few of them are genuine improvements on those that are already in cultivation and most disappear from nursery lists very quickly. However, there are some very good introductions that may be lost because they are currently unfashionable. Single-flowered fuchsias, i.e., those whose corolla consists of only four petals, usually make excellent exhibition plants because they bloom so profusely. Unfortunately exhibitors and those enthusiasts who belong to societies are still a small minority when it come to the fuchsia-buying public as a whole. The majority of growers want double flowers; the larger they are the better, and the size of blooms is perceived as an expression of quality. I am not at all critical of this preference as I admit to liking large-bloomed cultivars myself; I just wish that the splendid multi-flowering single types were appreciated by a wider range of the public than they are at present. The preference for large blooms is not just confined to Great Britain. Judging by the number of giant-flowered introductions that come from the U.S.A. and Australia the demand is just the same there. Although it may be slow, progress is being made in all spheres of fuchsia growing. Not only is there great hope of advancement for the present generation of growers, but there is the knowledge that future generations will appreciate our current achievements just as we marvel at the achievements of all those who have gone before us.

History, Botany, and Nomenclature

The vast majority of fuchsia species are found growing in the Americas so their story, as far as the western civilization is concerned, could only begin after the discovery and exploration of their homelands. It took some time before plant lovers fully appreciated the decorative quality of fuchsias, but when this occurred it created an explosion of interest that has spread around the world.

The reasons why fuchsias are so popular are diverse. The unusual shape of the flowers, like little ballerinas, fascinates some people, while others like their ease of propagation or free-flowering qualities. Whatever their attraction, millions of people now grow fuchsias in their greenhouses or gardens.

Right: "Stella Ann" is a typical member of the triphylla group of fuchsias, which is characterized by producing bunches of blooms at the end of the branches

Gardeners in Great Britain are particularly attracted to fuchsias, but perhaps this can be explained by the fact that they are one of the very few flowering shrubs that do better in a wet summer than a dry one. If the scientists' theories about global warming are true then perhaps this may change. Only time will tell.

History

The history of the fuschia dates back to the 17th Century when Father Charles Plumier, a French botanist and missionary, discovered one on a plant-hunting expedition. He named it after Leonhardt Fuchs (1501-66) who had held the chair of medicine at Tübingen University in southern Germany. (Plumier also named the *Begonia* after Michel Begon, the *Magnolia* after Professor Pierre Magnol, and the *Lobelia* after Matthias de Lobel.)

Plumier was born in 1646 in Marseilles. He was going to become a woodturner and engraver like his father, but joined the Catholic Church. In Rome he gained an interest in botany, and he developed a special interest in the healing properties of plants. He later returned to France and studied botany at the University of Aix-en-Provence.

He made at least three journeys to the West Indies at the end of the 17th Century, and to many of the French colonies in the Americas. On one of these missions his ship foundered and all his specimens, which probably included the first fuchsia, were lost. Plumier described and named this specimen *Fuchsia triphylla florecoccinea* from his notes that were sent to France by another ship that did arrive safely. These notes, published by Plumier in his book *Nova Plantarum Americanum Genera* (1703), were not very detailed, but the description and drawings enabled the Swedish naturalist Carl Linnaeus to create the genus *Fuchsia* in his *Species Plantarum* (1753). A pupil of Plumier later gave a full and accurate description of this plant, which has become known as *Fuchsia triphylla*.

Surprisingly, even after a lapse of 170 years no specimens had found their way back to Europe. Botanists began doubting if this plant actually existed. Then, in 1872, Thomas Hogg, an American working in the West Indies, collected seed from a plant found growing near Santo Domingo which turned out to be *F. triphylla*.

Although other species of fuchsia had been discovered, the first to reach England was a native of Brazil called *F. coccinea*. It was donated by Captain Firth to Kew Gardens in 1788. The same year a nurseryman called James Lee managed to acquire this plant, and propagated sufficient stock to offer it for sale in 1793. The plant was very popular, and other nurseries sponsored expeditions to find new species. On these trips the fuchsias *F. magellanica*, *F. fulgens*, *F. arborescens* and *F. lycoides* were discovered .

Today species have been found in South and Central America, Tahiti, and New Zealand, where fossilized fuchsia pollen has been found dating back approximately 30 million years. Despite this amazing find, the homeland for fuchsias is considered to be Central America.

Father Gregor Mendel is famous for discovering the laws of inheritance among plants. Although this breakthrough was achieved using peas, one of his favorite flowers was the fuchsia. He was elected an abbot in 1868 and he chose, as part of his coat of arms, a fuchsia flower.

Botanically the fuchsia is one of the 21 genera included in the order *Onagraceae*. The genus *Fuchsia* consists of about 100 species and is divided into several sections. Full details can be found in specialized works such as the *Revision of the Genus Fuchsia* by Dr. P. A. Munz (1943). The genus is diverse and ranges from *F. procumbens*, just a few centimeters high, to *F. excorticata*, which forms a tree which can grow up to 29 feet (8.8 m) high.

The majority of species are shrubby and inhabit cool mountain slopes with high rainfall, or dense forests and jungles. *F. tunariensis* is unusual because it lives as an epiphyte in the branches of trees or on rocks, and has tuberous roots. Although the uses of the species are mainly ornamental, the leaves and bark of *F. magellanica* are said to have medicinal properties, and the blue pollen of *F. excorticata* and *F. procumbens* have been used for facial decoration by Maori women.

06

Inuida multorum te exercuit vſque Voluntas,
Vera tuis creuit ſed Medicina ſcholis.
Herbas in primis noras, ϰ̀ φάρμακα πάοϛ̀ν,
Contrahere artifici ſenſáque lata modo.

Early hybridization

The first attempts at hybridization were made early in the 19th Century, but very little of this work was recorded. In 1840, by chance, a seedling was raised by a gardener in southern England that had a white tube and sepals, and a purple corolla. The white tube was a completely new color break and the cultivar was distributed under the name "Venus Victrix." It is generally thought that the majority of hybrids grown today with a white tube include this plant in their parentage.

Apparently this seedling arose by chance and was not the result of a deliberate breeding program. But the plant itself has little else to commend it because its growth is straggly and weak. This is one of many instances in the history of the fuchsia where chance has played a major part in its development.

The first double-flowered fuchsia was raised in 1850 by a Mr. Story, a nurseryman in southwest England. He

Right: The French fuchsia grower John Emile Lemoine. who raised over 400 cultivars

Below: The English grower James Lye with a collection of his prize fuchsias

also raised the first fuchsia with a striped corolla which has apparently now been lost to cultivation. By this time fuchsias were being grown and hybridized throughout Europe, particularly in France, Germany, and Belgium.

At around the turn of the century, the French grower Lemoine named over 400 cultivars and some, such as "Monsieur Thibaut" and "Abbé Farges," are still very popular. Another important French introduction was "Bon Accorde," raised by Crousse in 1861. It was the

first known cultivar to hold its flowers upward. The Belgian grower Cornelissen raised "Madame Cornelissen," a hardy cultivar with red-and-white blooms (it is still widely available).

The German nurserymen Rehnelt and Bonstedt raised many hybrids from Plumier's *F. triphylla*. As a group they are easily distinguishable from other

LEAF NODE

OVARY

TUBE

SEPALS

COROLLA

FILAMENTS

ANTHERS

STIGMA

cultivars as they closely resemble *F. triphylla*, having long flowers in bunches and large, mainly olive-green leaves with red undersides. This distinct group of plants are now called the *triphylla* hybrids.

Peter Fitzgerald (1808-1880) was a knight of Kerry in Ireland and was responsible for developing the Glanlean Estate. He wrote letters to the London *Times* newspaper on the virtues of the fuchsia as a shelter belt.(The Irish name for the fuchsia means "Tears of God.")

In England, fuchsias reached their peak of popularity in the last half of the 19th Century. Time and wealth meant the landed gentry could afford to build heated greenhouses and conservatories on an unprecedented scale. The Victorians often used fuchsias as cut flowers, the beautiful arching branches being well suited to the multi-tiered containers and epergnes then popular.

They could also afford to employ dozens of gardeners to fashion these plants into myriads of decorative shapes. The most famous gardener of all was James Lye who, in 1866, was described as the champion fuchsia grower in the

"Swingtime" was raised by Horace Tiret in San Francisco (1950). It is still one of the all-time favorites and is said to be a cross between "Titanic" (Reiter, 1946) and "Yuletide" (Tiret, 1948)

west of England. He also raised a number of fine cultivars such as "Lyes Unique," which has a white tube and sepals, and a pale orange corolla. In 1866 Lyes' daughter married George Bright, another superb grower and exhibitor of fuchsias.

Within a few years, Bright was exhibiting specimens that were said to be even better than Lyes'. Bright also raised the cultivar "Coachman," which even today is regarded as one of the best of the orange-flowered hybrids.

Edward Banks, living near Deal in the south of England, was a prolific hybridizer who raised many fine new plants from about 1852-1886. He died in 1910 at the age of 90. His death roughly coincided with the decline of interest in fuchsias in Great Britain. Two of his introductions, "Rose of Denmark" and "Rose of Castile," are particular favorites of the author. "Forget-Me-Not," raised in 1866, was chosen by the British Fuchsia Society as its emblem.

Toward the end of the last century fuchsias commanded high prices. In Cannell's catalog, novelties were priced at three shillings and six pence. To put this in perspective, an ordinary worker of the time would have been able to buy only three with his average weekly wage.

The fuchsia's popularity continued right up to the First World War when labor became scarce, and greenhouses were used for food production rather than flowers. After the war fuchsias became synonymous with a bygone age and their popularity began to diminish.

The story continues in California where the American Fuchsia Society was founded in 1929. Soon after its inauguration members of the society traveled to Europe to collect cultivars to take back to the U.S.A. The plants were hybridized and used to create many new and varied forms, in a range of pastel colors, that had not been seen before. H.M. Tiret of San Francisco raised great classics such as

"Jack Shahan," "Swingtime" and "Leonora," while Gus Niederholzer, also from San Francisco, raised over 130 new cultivars, including "Collingwood." Victor Reiter introduced "Jeane" (often misspelled "Genie" or "Genii"), a marvelous hardy cultivar with red-and-purple flowers and lemon-yellow leaves.

More recently Edward Paskesen, who died in 1979, raised "Bicentennial," a double orange-and-purple hanging-basket cultivar to commemorate the American bicentennial.

The British Fuchsia Society was founded in 1938 just before the Second World War. Despite the difficulties this imposed, the society published a yearbook to keep members interested.

In the 1950s British growers, seeing the new American creations, began importing them enthusiastically. These novelties created a great deal of interest and were responsible for the second great wave of popularity in Great Britain, which still remains undiminished.

"Jeane," often misspelled "Genie" or "Genii," was raised by Reiter (1951). The blooms are very freely produced for a cultivar that also has ornamental lemon-yellow foliage. It is accepted as hardy by the British Fuchsia Society

Naming Procedures

In 1967, The American Fuchsia Society was appointed by The International Society for Horticultural Science as the international authority for fuchsia registration and nomenclature. Every new cultivar submitted to them is described, given a unique number, and the proposed name is checked to avoid duplication. The registration procedure is voluntary, so name duplications do still occur – for example, "Powder Puff," raised by Hodges in the U.S.A. (1953), and the hardy cultivar of the same name raised by Tabraham in Great Britain (1976).

There are many hybridizers now operating around the world, with as many amateurs as professional nursery experts. The most active countries are the U.S.A., Great Britain, and Holland, with notable contributions from Australia among others. It is not known how many fuchsia cultivars have been named, but they must number over 7,000. Since there can only be a relatively small number of distinctly different color combinations or forms, there is a great deal of duplication. Some cultivars are so similar that it is almost impossible to distinguish between them; virtually all new varieties are similar to something that already exists. There are more names than distinctly different hybrids. Just compare the pink-and-white blooms of "Cotton Candy" and "Torville and Dean." Furthermore, the new hybrids are often inferior to the old.

Since growers are always looking for something new, the pressure is on nurseries to produce something different each year, even if it is just the name! Unfortunately the situation is made worse by amateur hybridists who naturally think that their own red-and-purple seedling is much better than the thousands that have been named before.

There are still many goals to be achieved – the flower size of hardy fuchsias could be improved, and we are still looking for a non-fading blue bloom, and perhaps that elusive, pure buttercup-yellow fuchsia will be with us before too long.

Cultivating Fuchsias

Many of the recommendations in this chapter relate to growing fuchsias in a greenhouse because controlling the temperature and humidity is not necessary, or even possible, outside. Some of the topics covered include temperature, light, and humidity,

Right: "Kegworth Carnival" was raised by H. Smith of Kegworth in Derbyshire, England (1978). The color of the blooms is very similar to the single flowered "Duchess of Albany" raised by Rundle in Britain (1891).

but while they are discussed separately, they are closely interrelated.

In summer, when light levels are high, the temperature rises and relative humidity falls. To prevent the atmosphere from becoming too dry, the pathways in the greenhouse should be sprayed with water to create the amount of humidity that fuchsias require. At the height of summer this method probably will not be sufficient; so light levels should be reduced by

shading, which in turn lowers the internal temperature and increases relative humidity. Conversely, in winter, when light levels and temperatures are low, the humidity may be too high, and dry heating will be necessary to compensate. Note that heaters that burn fuels such as kerosene or gas, and which do not have a flue leading outside, actually increase the atmospheric moisture.

Temperature

Fuchsias naturally inhabit areas with climates ranging from tropical or sub-tropical in Central America, to the chilling landscapes at the tip of South America. Although they are not the only areas where species are found, these markedly different climatic conditions give an indication of the relative hardiness of the hybrids raised from them. For example, the triphylla group, which are mainly crosses between two tropical species, *F. triphylla* and *F. fulgens*, resemble their parents and need warm conditions – a minimum of 50°F (10°C) if they are to survive over the winter. Hybrids such as "Hawkshead," one of whose parents is *F. magellanica* var. *molinae* from Chile or Argentina, can withstand much colder conditions.

The large majority of hybrids fall between these two extremes and in summer, when they are growing and flowering, they prefer temperatures of 60-75°F (16-24°C) with a humid atmosphere. However, provided the plants are kept drier than usual, they can withstand considerably lower temperatures than that, and can similarly survive much higher temperatures if they are regularly sprayed overhead with clean water.

At temperatures below 41-46°F (5-8°C) fuchsias become dormant and most, if not all, the leaves will fall. If the temperature is allowed to drop below freezing point, 32°F (0°C), most die. High temperatures, above 80°F (27°C), are tolerated, provided the atmosphere is kept moist by spraying all paths and bare surfaces with water; otherwise there is a danger that the flower buds will abort and the leaves fall prematurely. Such conditions also weaken the plants so they become prey to pests, particularly red spider mite.

Opposite: "Marcus Graham" is currently one of the most sought after fuchsias when it was shown on a national television program

The only way to determine temperature accurately is by using a thermometer. A conventional thermometer will only give you the temperature at the time it is actually read, and as minimum temperatures usually occur in the early hours of the morning, exceptionally low readings can go unnoticed. Most garden centers have inexpensive maximum-minimum thermometers. They automatically record the daily maximum and minimum temperatures reached since the thermometer was last read and reset. These instruments are essential in the greenhouse, and are not just an optional extra.

Outdoors, fuchsias are much hardier when planted directly in the ground than in tubs or pots. Although in severe weather all the stems above ground will be killed, many of the hardier plants will regrow from parts of the stems under the surface which have been protected by the soil above them. The soil in pots and tubs can easily freeze solid in winter. Any fuchsias planted in them, regardless of hardiness, will die.

One of the attractions of fuchsias is that they can be trained into many different shapes, such as fans, pillars, and standards. Even if these plants are grown using the hardiest of cultivars they still need frost protection in winter, or they will be lost. They may survive at or below soil level, but the carefully crafted aerial stems will have perished. Fuchsias that have been elaborately trained are costly to buy because of the large amount of work involved in growing them. As a safeguard they should be kept at a minimum temperature of 50°F (10°C) at all times.

In most areas where fuchsias are grown, the summer conditions are suitable for outdoor cultivation. Many growers put all their plants outside at this time because they need considerably less attention, and to a great extent look after themselves. Obviously all tender plants must be returned to the greenhouse before the first frost. The big problem is that what comes out never quite fits back in again!

Light

Fuchsias need good light and some direct sunshine to develop properly. However, there are a few pale- or yellow-leafed cultivars that need protection from strong sunlight and are best kept lightly shaded, both in the greenhouse and the garden. However, they are an exception, and there are many similar cultivars that revel in full light.

In general, the only harmful effects of strong light are the result of the accompanying high temperatures and reduced humidity levels that this brings. In summer, inside the greenhouse, high temperatures can burn leaves and, particularly, buds; the resultant low humidity can also cause buds to drop before they have opened. The solution is to shade the greenhouse or, if the weather is settled, move the plants into the garden where conditions are cooler. If in doubt, always err towards too much light rather than too little. Poor light makes fuchsias grow weakly and reduces the number of blooms.

Light also affects the color of fuchsia blooms. White-flowered fuchsias, particularly if slightly starved, bloom with pink overtones when grown in full sun. To approach a pure white you need to keep all white-flowered cultivars slightly shaded. Annabelle Stubbs, the well-known American raiser of so many beautiful cultivars, has apparently said that "fuchsias are not shade loving plants, loving all the light possible, without burning." These are the conditions in which her plants are grown at her nursery at Fort Bragg in California. One of her superb introductions is "Pink Marshmallow," which in England has but the faintest tinge of pink on an otherwise unblemished pure-white bloom. As its name implies, it obviously has a much deeper color in its homeland. This variation must be due to the differences in cultivation and light levels between California and England. Similarly, many darker-colored fuchsias change their colors quite dramatically in response to feeding and light intensity.

Humidity

The amount of water vapor present in air is measured as a percentage of the total it can hold at saturation point. For example, if the air is fully saturated with moisture it is at a state of 100 percent relative humidity at that temperature. Plants growing in these conditions absorb as much water from the atmosphere as they lose by evaporation. A dynamic equilibrium is maintained. However, if the temperature rises, the air is now able to hold more moisture. Provided the amount of water present in the air remains the same, the relative humidity falls and the plants start to lose water through their leaves. If the temperature continues to rise and no attempt is made to increase the atmospheric moisture, the relative humidity continues to fall and may reach a critical level. Eventually the point comes when plants are expiring water so fast that their root and vascular systems cannot cope. Consequently they start to wilt, even though they have plenty of moisture around their roots. This is the reason why paths and any other bare surfaces should be sprayed liberally with water in hot weather; the evaporation increases the relative humidity, and relieves the plants from stress.

In a stable environment plants keep a natural equilibrium between the size of their root systems and the size and number of stems and leaves above-ground. The root system is large enough to draw up sufficient water to compensate for the normal transpiration loss through the leaves. In effect, the size of the root system is influenced by the average relative humidity and the rate of airflow around the plants.

In early spring, when it is still cold outside, the greenhouse ventilators are rarely opened and the internal humidity is high, and air movement low. Sooner or later warm spring sunshine will force you to open the ventilators and the relatively still and cosy microclimate inside the greenhouse suddenly changes. The plants are subjected to a steady flow of air which rapidly carries moisture away from the leaves. At this point the rate of water loss from the leaves sometimes exceeds the root systems' ability to sustain them and, though the soil is moist, the plants droop.

Opposite: "Orange Drops." Orange-flowered hybrids are always more troublesome to grow than those of other colors. This one is about the best currently available as it is more tolerant than most to adverse conditions and very free-flowering

The answer is not to increase watering at the roots, which will do more harm than good, but to increase atmospheric moisture by lightly spraying the foliage with clean water to prevent excessive wilting. After a time the plants respond to the changes by growing larger root systems, and they harden themselves to reduce water loss.

The hardening process involves a reduction of the number and size of new leaves, which reduces the area of evaporation. It also alters their physical structure. These natural processes may take a few weeks. The best course of action is to anticipate this problem by opening the greenhouse ventilators on every possible occasion, even if only a crack, so that the plants gradually become accustomed to the seasonal changes outside.

Plants grown in unsuitable conditions are placed under a great strain. The struggle for existence can predispose them to attacks by pests and diseases. Greenhouse red spider mite revels in hot, dry conditions and can cause considerable damage. If leaves begin to fall from fuchsias in summer in abnormal numbers, lack of humidity with secondary damage by this pernicious pest should always be suspected.

Fuchsias react badly to sudden changes in humidity. For example, beautiful specimens can be grown in a well managed greenhouse but if you move them into the livingroom to admire them more closely, unpleasant things can start to happen. First, often overnight, most of the buds fall, and if the plants are not returned to the greenhouse, leaves start to fall as well. Some cultivars are more tolerant of being moved around than others, and make reasonable houseplants provided they are hardened in the greenhouse by carefully restricting watering, and by giving good ventilation. Nonetheless, they are best returned to the greenhouse after a few weeks to prevent any deterioration.

Generally speaking, fuchsias do not make very good houseplants. The humidity in the average home is too low, and the plants also drip copious amounts of sugary nectar which can badly damage furniture. It must also be said that the author has been scolded on this point by Dutch friends who argue that if more plants were grown in the

home, the transpiration from their leaves would increase atmospheric humidity. This, in turn, would counteract the bad effects of central heating and create a better environment for both people and plants to live in. Perhaps they have a point, or are they trying to sell us more house plants?

The nectar dripping from fuchsia flowers, apart from damaging furniture, also falls onto the foliage leaving a shiny, sticky residue. With age this deposit usually develops into an unsightly black mold that can be mistaken for disease. Plants growing outdoors have the deposits washed away by rain, but in the greenhouse you must spray the foliage to clean away the deposits. This also helps to prevent wilting. However, take care not to spray water over the flowers as they are easily marked. This may not be too serious for the average grower, but could be of vital importance to an exhibitor.

Watering

Fuchsias in pots need regular watering, and they should not be allowed to dry out completely at any time except when the temperature falls below that needed to sustain growth, i.e., 44°F (7°C). Large plants, particularly when in full flower, are difficult to overwater. However, if the soil is moist it is better to leave them alone until the surface starts to become paler in color. In hot weather, mature plants may need watering several times a day, but only once or twice a week if the weather is damp and cool. Plants under cover need more water than those in the open, which benefit from natural rainfall.

Young rooted cuttings that have just been potted need very careful weaning as they are at a very vulnerable time. The main problem is overwatering. The best advice is to keep the plants just on the verge of becoming dry. This requires frequent observation in hot weather when a few hours' neglect can render them excessively dry. If they are kept too wet at this stage there may be unacceptably high losses, or the soil will become sour and green on the surface, hindering future development. One often hears the sorry tale, "I bought six fuchsias and treated them all exactly the same and two have died. But *why*?" The answer is simple; they should *not* have been treated exactly the same. Different cultivars vary greatly in their requirements, and even among plants of the same cultivar there can be variations in vigor. If they are not given individual treatment at this critical phase, losses may be unacceptably high.

Once the plants are well established they can survive a degree of overwatering. Under these conditions, provided they are well-fed, they will grow luxuriantly, often to excess. This does not seem to affect unduly the total number of blooms, but the leaves may grow unnaturally large and hide the flowers. The internodal distance (the distance between pairs of leaves) will also lengthen. But the main problem is that the plants become soft and less able to withstand a sudden spell of hot, dry weather, or other adverse conditions. Young plants need to grow rapidly so a little, carefully controlled, luxuriant growth is not a fault at this stage, but it must be tempered with careful watering and a gradual drying-out period to bring them to healthy maturity.

If you do not have a local specialty nursery, you may have to buy new cultivars by mail order. Plants sent by mail have to be securely packaged, which usually means they are going to be in the dark for at least 24 hours. It is ironic that the healthiest plants, because of their vigorous growth, deteriorate most rapidly in these conditions. The only answer is to order from a reliable supplier and ensure that the plants are sent by the fastest delivery service.

On arrival, plants that have been in the dark for more than three days may be distressed. In any case, as the conditions in your own greenhouse may be very different from the suppliers', a short settling-in period is necessary.

Keep the plants shaded for a few days and, if the weather is hot, spray them frequently with clean water. If the nursery has sent bareroot cuttings, i.e., plants not supplied with the rootball intact, they must be immediately potted. However, those sent in individual containers can be allowed to acclimatize for a few days before being repotted.

The quality of water used is not usually critical; if it is fit for drinking it should suffice. Soft and hard water are both equally suitable for watering the soil, but avoid spraying hard water over the plants as the salts it contains leave unsightly marks on the foliage. Clean rainwater can be used for all purposes and, as it should be free of dissolved salts, is particularly good for spraying.

Storage tanks or rainwater barrels must be cleaned annually to remove rotting leaves and other debris. If they are not, you end up with what many authorities describe as disease soup! The use of contaminated water is the source of many fungal and bacterial infections, particularly those that cause root rot.

Watering plants by hand is always best, provided you have the time. Every plant will get individual attention so the overall quality improves. If you have a large collection of plants this may be too time-consuming and growing fuchsias may become a chore. Luckily, there are a number of ways to automate the process, one of the most popular and successful being capillary watering.

This involves standing the plants on a specially manufactured absorbent cloth which lies on a sheet of plastic to prevent the water from draining away. The matting is kept moist and the plants take up the water by capillary action.

A number of manufacturers market complete kits with a moisture sensor and water tank, so the whole procedure can be fully automated. Once well tested, such systems can be left for as long as two weeks. This system will only work for pots smaller than about 5 in. (12.5 cm) in diameter, as there is a limit to the height that the water can be drawn up by capillarity.

Plants in larger pots can have small, individual drip lines inserted into their containers. This can also be automated using a sensor and control box. Complete systems are available from various manufacturers and large garden centers. These labor-saving devices work well, but it takes time to get all the adjustments working correctly. Do not expect perfect results immediately. Before being placed on capillary matting, it is always best to hand-water small and newly potted plants until they are well established.

Some growers say that watering the soil surface gives different results from letting the soil draw up water from below. The aim should be to supply enough water to just wet the root ball, no more, no less, so using either method should give the same result. When using the capillary method there will be extra humidity created by the wet matting. This can be an advantage or disadvantage depending on whether the temperature is high or low.

Remember also that any fertilizer dissolved from the compost will be returned via the capillary matting, while hand watering on open staging allows nutrients to be washed away. This difference means that the rate and level of feeding should be slightly adjusted depending on the method used.

"Brookwood Belle" is the best red-and-white flowering cultivar to be raised in recent years

Nutrition and Feeding

This is undoubtedly one of the most misunderstood aspects of fuchsia culture, and it is made worse by the fact that many books are confusing and contradictory on the subject. For this reason this aspect is described in detail.

In a similar manner to animals, many plant processes are controlled by hormones. Plant hormones are given the special name of auxins. The various levels of particular auxins control the growth phases of the plant, and dictate when it grows and when it flowers. The processes are complex and not yet fully understood, even by scientists, so what follows is therefore a simplification.

At an early stage in the spring, just as the plants are breaking into new growth, the tendency to produce flower buds is kept in check by the auxins so that they can make new leaves and stems as quickly as possible. The leaves absorb the energy of sunlight and change the mineral salts obtained from the soil and carbon dioxide from the air to make food for new growth. This is the process of photosynthesis which is carried out by chlorophyll, the green coloring matter of plants. Obviously in the early stages of growth the plant needs to increase its size as quickly as possible and the formation of flowers would slow this process down. Cuttings taken from plants at this stage, i.e., without flower buds being pre-

sent, root very easily. After a while the effect of the auxin controlling this aspect of growth begins to wane, perhaps controlled by the size of the plant but certainly by the length of day and temperature.

At this point another auxin or chemical trigger responsible for the formation of blooms takes over, and flower buds start to grow. It should be noted at this stage that when this occurs the extension of stems slows dramatically and the plants increase in size relatively slowly. Cuttings taken from them at this stage are much more difficult to root. The above describes a process that occurs naturally and is not normally controlled by the grower. However, research has shown that the flowering phase can be advanced by artificially illuminating the plants to increase day length. This aspect is ignored by all but a few commercial growers.

Many books discuss the growing and flowering cycle in relation to the type of fertilizer used. Nitrogenous fertilizers are said to promote growth, and those high in potassium to prevent flowering. While this is true, the overall effect of these fertilizers is small compared to the role of the auxins. The following is a fairly typical example of the life of a fuchsia plant, starting with a rooted cutting, explained with reference to its changes in hormone levels and with the use of various fertilizers.

The cutting is planted in potting compost in a

small container in spring. Potting compost contains a high level of nitrogen which, with the natural growth hormone, creates very rapid growth. Carefully controlled watering is given to ensure that the growth does not become too soft. When the plant fills the small pot with roots, it is potted into a larger container with fresh potting compost. The growth at this stage is sustained by increasing the pot size, not by feeding.

When the plant has reestablished itself, growth continues rapidly and each stem grows by several centimeters a week. After repotting again into a 6 in. (15 cm) pot, the plant is near flowering size. At this time, depending on the vigor of the particular cultivar, it is allowed to flower in this pot or is moved to a larger one.

The plant hormones responsible for growth are now having less effect as they are being replaced by those controlling flower formation. The result is that stem and leaf growth starts to decline as buds start to form. At the same time the plant has used up most of the nutrients in the compost and feeding begins.

If it is being entered for an exhibition and the date of the show is nowhere near, there is little point in allowing it to flower now. The flower buds should be picked off as soon as they are large enough to handle, and the plant fed with a high-nitrogen fertilizer to encourage as much growth as possible. This will not be great as it is working against the flower-bearing hormonal influences, but as good big fuchsias win more prizes than good little ones, the difference may be crucial.

All buds are left on for about four to six weeks before the date of the show to allow the plant to come into full bloom. About eight weeks before the show a change to a high-potassium food is made. This hardens the growth by thickening the cell walls so that the blooms will not bruise when being transported, and also helps intensify the color. Following this course of action ensures that the plant will be at its optimum size with the maximum number of blooms on show day.

In the few weeks before the show, as all the plant's energy is being used to form flowers, the stems will hardly extend at all. After the initial mass of blooms there will be very few flowers to follow. This is because new flower buds are only formed as the stems elongate, and this does not happen because all the plant's energy is being channeled into producing the mass of new blooms. After a few weeks the plant begins flowering again as lateral growth recommences.

Alternatively, if the plant is intended for general decoration, it is given a high-nitrogen food throughout the flowering period. This keeps the stem tips growing so that a constant, but slightly less profuse, display of blooms appears. Because the plant does not have to be transported to a show, the hardening effect of the high potassium food is not needed. In fact the only reason for a high potassium food, when the plant is in early vegetative growth, is to speed up the first crop of flower buds. But since flower formation is mainly controlled by the level of auxins, which themselves are controlled by the seasons, there is little advantage to be gained.

Plant fertilizers contain three main elements: nitrogen, phosphorus, and potassium (often called potash), with a number of minor or trace elements such as magnesium and iron. The analysis of a fertilizer is printed on the package or bottle. A typical analysis will appear as:-

Nitrogen (N)	10.0%
Phosphorus	5.0%
(P as P_2O_5)	
Potassium	10.0%
(K as K_2O)	

In a different way this fertilizer could be described as a (10:5:10) NPK or even a (2:1:2) NPK formulation. A product with analysis 20:10:20 NPK or 30:15:30 NPK or any of the others just mentioned will give identical results when used at the correct dilution; they are all the same!

The concentration of fertilizers supplied by different manufacturers varies, particularly between those sold as solids or as liquids. Each must be applied at the correct strength, according to the manufacturer's instructions. As a general guide, apply fertilizer at the recommended rate at every fifth watering. In other words, if you have to water your plants every day you should feed them every five days, and if you only need to water once a week, feed every five weeks. But remember, plants growing on capillary matting may need less feeding than those on open staging.

The process of feeding plants places quite a burden on the grower. Underfeeding is harmful because the quality of the plant slowly declines. However, if you are observant, this gradual decline will be noticed at an early stage and the process can be reversed, either by repotting or by increasing the amount, or frequency, of feeding. Overfeeding is even worse because the plant continues to look very healthy until the roots suddenly die. It is then too late to save the plant. Small meters are available from some garden centers that measure the conductivity of the soil. This is a guide to the total amount of nutrients dissolved in the soil water, and indicates whether you need to apply more fertilizer. These devices are not always reliable, and commercial growers use laboratory services to give more accurate information.

In the last two decades, slow-release fertilizers have been developed. They consist of small beads of a complete fertilizer coated with a special, plastic compound. The plastic coating, which also contains trace elements, allows the fertilizer to dissolve slowly at a rate controlled only by temperature. This means that the higher the temperature, the faster the fertilizer is released, which nicely suits the way plants naturally grow.

Composts containing these fertilizers feed plants automatically for many months, so it is only necessary to feed them occasionally, and then only at

the end of the season when the slow-release fertilizer is becoming exhausted. Although they were originally invented for commercial use, the most popular of these products is now available in small packs from some retailers. They are quite costly, but the results obtained by using them are very worthwhile. The rate of use of this special fertilizer is given on the packs and you have to add it yourself to your favorite compost.

Once mixed, composts containing slow-release fertilizers start to work within a short time, and if the compost is not used quickly the available nutrients soon build up to dangerous levels. This means that pre-mixed products have too short a shelf life to be stocked by garden centers. All composts should be used up within two weeks after you have added the slow-release fertilizer to it.

The difference between the various fertilizer formulations is not the absolute amount of nutrient that each contains, but the amount of one nutrient compared to another. Only the relative amounts of nitrogen and potassium are normally considered. Take the example 10:5:10 NPK. The nitrogen and potassium concentrations are the same, so the fertilizer is said to be balanced. It is a good, general purpose product. A 20:5:10

Organic matter (composted leaves or peat) is a basic ingredient for a home-made soil

NPK fertilizer is a high-nitrogen formulation because it contains twice as much nitrogen as potassium. Similarly a 10:5:20 NPK formulation is a high-potassium fertilizer, containing twice as much potassium as nitrogen. 30:5:10 or 10:5:30 fertilizers are also made, but being far from balanced they should be used with care or more harm will be done than good.

Both the nitrogen and potassium content of a fertilizer is very soluble, and is easily washed away in the water draining out of the pots, unless you are using capillary matting. Phosphorus is normally supplied in the form of phosphates which combine with chalk in the compost to form a relatively insoluble material. For this reason, particularly if your water supply is hard, a formulation without phosphorus, such as 10:0:20, may be all that is needed as the amount supplied by the potting compost will be sufficient. In any event, excess phosphorus is not particularly harmful to fuchsias.

It has already been said that it is the ratio of one nutrient to another which is important, not their actual concentrations. For example, there is a relationship between potassium and magnesium. If you continually feed a fertilizer that contains a very high level of potassium you can upset the balance so much as to induce magnesium-deficiency symptoms, although there may still be plenty of magnesium present in the soil. The identification of mineral deficiencies by the appearance of leaves is very complex and the symptoms vary greatly from species to species. This aspect of plant culture is difficult to master, so if there is any doubt, repotting the plants is generally the best way to solve nutritional difficulties.

Alternatively, plants can have their soil balls immersed in a large volume of water for several hours. This will dissolve away most of the soluble nutrients. The plants can then be soaked in a fresh solution of good-quality, liquid food, which should restore the correct balance of nutrients. The food must contain all the trace elements, as they will also have been removed in the

soaking. Some people water their plants by standing them in a bowl of water and then allowing them to drain. This is not a good idea, as a lot of soil nutrients will be lost and the remainder may become unbalanced due to the differences in solubility of the various fertilizer components.

Early in the morning you may notice that some fuchsias, when very moist at the roots, collect droplets of water round the leaf edges. This is most noticeable in greenhouse plants. The droplets vanish as the temperature rises, but in some cases a nasty, powdery deposit is left. Most experts say it is caused by overfeeding, but that is not usually true. The nitrogen content of a fertilizer is mostly present in the form of nitrates or ammonium salts, both of which, in excess, quickly kill plant roots. The symptoms of overfeeding are wilting, followed by rapid death of the whole plant. The real cause of the leaf spots is a buildup of waste material in the compost.

Fertilizers often contain elements that are not needed by plants. For example, potassium may be supplied as potassium sulphate which leaves unwanted sulphates in the soil. These and other unused fertilizer components gradually build up each time the plant is fed. Although the plants absorb some of these compounds, they are not needed for growth so they expel them any way they can.

Grit or sharp sand is another basic ingredient for a homemade soil

Proprietary soil improvers, such as this calcined clay or crushed pumice, can be added to the mix to ensure that it remains absorbent and free-draining for a long period. They can also be used alone if extra care can be taken when watering

Fertilizer manufacturers can minimize this problem by the use of more expensive ingredients such as potassium nitrate, which can be totally utilized by plants. If the buildup of waste products is a constant problem, change to a better-quality fertilizer. Generally, the more expensive fertilizers are well worth the extra money.

If you are an organic gardener and do not want to use chemical fertilizers, you may have a favorite way of supplying the necessary nutrients. Some fertilizers made from natural sources, such as seaweed, do have an analysis printed on the package. However, homemade manure water contains an unknown level of nutrients and, in my experience, does not work well when fed to potted plants. Growing plants in pots is unnatural, so for the best results unnatural cultivation methods have to be used.

Soils and Potting

For the best results, the compost used for potting plants has to have a carefully defined structure. It must also contain the correct levels of major and trace elements, and have a suitable pH. Garden soil on its own is unlikely to be of any use. The level of nutrients it contains will be insufficient and, unless you are very lucky, its vital air/water ratio will be wrong for use in containers. It is also likely to contain diseases or even worms that play havoc with the roots when confined in a pot. It is also a good way to get vine weevil larvae into the greenhouse. This pest is very destructive and notoriously difficult to control.

In the garden, plant roots have a large volume of soil to work through and can seek out nutrients from a surprisingly wide area. Plants growing in containers do not have this luxury, so the soil in which they are growing has to be very special.

Do not waste your time using anything except a good potting compost especially designed for the purpose. Do not confuse garden compost, made from rotted plant remains and kitchen scraps, with potting compost. The two materials are very different. Potting compost is designed for use with established or well-rooted plants. Do not use it for starting cuttings or sowing seeds or the results will be poor. General-purpose composts can be used for both, but as the nutrient content is a compromise, they are normally adequate for seed sowing, but need an additional feeding when used for established plants. However, these composts are ideal for potting when they are supplemented with the addition of a slow-release fertilizer.

Potting composts, or seed-sowing and cuttings composts for that matter, can be divided into two categories: those that contain soil and those that do not. The most famous soil-based composts are those developed at the John Innes Institute in England. These composts consist of good loam, which is basically rotted turf from old pastureland, gritty sand, peat, and special fertilizers. These composts can give superb results but unfortunately they are only as good as the quality of loam used, and today this is a scarce and very variable commodity.

**Opposite:
The illustration shows two cuttings growing in peat pots. The fresh white roots that have penetrated to the outside are a good indication that they are now ready to be potted into larger containers. Before planting, pots of this type should have the rim carefully removed and care must be taken to avoid damaging the roots**

The traditional method for producing loam was to cut the turf from old pastures in the autumn and stack it grass-side down, putting rotted horse manure between each layer. The following spring this was mixed, shredded, and partially sterilized by steam before being used. Today, the rich old pastureland and horse manure are rarely available, and the quality of the compost suffers. Recent commercial samples rarely, if ever, match the original specifications, and modern soil-less composts usually give the best results. However, soil-based composts still have their uses. Some trained fuchsias, such as standards, need a stake in the compost. This is given much more support by soil than by the spongy, soil-less mixtures. Soil-based composts are also easier to manage; they re-wet more easily if they become dry, and feeding plants in them is a lot less critical.

The soilless composts, first formulated by the University of California, consisted of a fertilized mix of peat and sand. Over the decades research has refined these products,

and they generally give very good results. The major ingredient is usually peat, and as this is a much less variable product than loam, the quality of soil-less composts is more constant from batch to batch. Peat is also one of the earth's most plentiful materials, and there are immense reserves for the future. A large part of Europe, extending from Norway and Sweden right across the massive areas of the old Soviet Union, largely consist of peat.

However, there are some sensitive areas that need special protection, so environmental agencies, governments, and manufacturers are protecting the most important wildlife areas from any permanent damage caused by its

composts only have a life of about six weeks after which, if they are not used, they start to become toxic to plants. At the time of manufacture all composts have their pH (acidity or alkalinity) adjusted to the optimum level. The correct pH is critical because it controls the way that various elements in the soil become available to the plants. Many gardeners know that some plants will not grow in acid soils. This is because there are substances such as manganese and aluminum present in soils which only become poisonous in acid conditions. Similarly it also makes some essential plant nutrients such as iron more available, which is why some plants lack iron when growing in alkaline soils.

extraction. Because there has been a campaign by some environmentalists to stop the use of peat entirely, peat-free composts are now commercially available. They are mostly based on coir (coconut fiber), shredded bark, or various other waste products. On average they are still inferior to peat-based composts, and more research is needed regarding their use and preparation. There are also fears that some of those based on recycled materials are actually damaging the environment by the spread of toxic metals.

All composts intended for growing plants are very complex, and it is always better to buy a well-known commercial product than to use a homemade one. The only exception is to buy the components as a kit and add them to a mix of peat and sand. Generally they give good results because they have been well researched and tested.

Unused soilless composts, providing they do not get wet, last quite a long time. John Innes'

Above: The two cuttings are well rooted and ready for potting into larger containers

Right: This shows the two cuttings illustrated above after they have been potted in larger containers. Note the small canes that have been inserted to provide support to the stems

The whole process is very complicated. My best advice is to buy a commercial brand and trust that the manufacturer has determined the best compromise to these problems for you.

Finally, we come to soil buffering. Plants can only take up nutrients through their roots as a solution in water. If all the nutrients present in potting compost were in solution at the same time their concentration would be high enough to kill a plant's roots. Soil has a great buffering effect and can lock up most of the nutrients, leaving a relatively small amount in the soil water. This small amount is kept at a constant level, so when the plants take up some nutrients through their roots, more is released by the soil to take its place. This intereaction is called the soil buffering effect. Soil (loam) is much more effective in this respect than peat or other soilless substitutes, and for this reason you can overfeed or underfeed plants growing in it to a greater extent without causing harm.

Fuchsias are exceptionally tolerant plants. Provided they are kept within reasonable limits they are not fussy about the type of compost in which they are grown, soil pH, or the level of nutrients. This means that the standard proprietary potting composts, and the average plant-feeding instructions on fertilizer packages, will suit fuchsias admirably.

Plants in pots must be planted at the correct depth. All of the root system must be below soil level and leaves must not touch the soil surface or they may rot

Young plants, as they increase in size, need to be repotted without disturbing the soil ball. Always do this in small steps so that the roots can quickly penetrate all the new soil and prevent it from staying wet for long periods, or it will become sour. Choose a container about 2 in. (5 cm) larger than the previous one, and pour the soil around the roots while tapping the pot, to settle it in. Soilless compost should only be tamped down enough to ensure that no air pockets are present. Soil-based composts need to be firmed in the pot slightly more. The air-to-water ratio in a compost is critical, and by over-firming

Above: This shows a cutting about 6-8 weeks after repotting in a larger pot. It is now ready for repotting again into a still-larger pot

Right: The illustration shows the plants above after being moved from a 4¼ in. (10 cm), to a 6 in. (15 cm) pot. If necessary, larger canes should be inserted to provide extra support to the stems

you alter this ratio to the plant's detriment. Always follow the printed instructions on bags of compost.

Old plants, particularly those grown in pots from year to year, occasionally need repotting or potting back. Repotting means carefully knocking the plant out of its pot and, without doing too much damage, removing as much of the old soil from the roots as possible, and then replanting in the same size pot with fresh compost. After careful watering the plant will be greatly invigorated.

This procedure is usually performed on mature plants in the spring just as they start new growth. If a lot of the roots are dead it is better to pot the plant back into a smaller container with fresh compost in the hope it will recover. Plants growing in soilless composts will benefit from repotting every spring, but those in soil-based composts need repotting much less frequently and can be sustained by feeding for at least two seasons.

These days most pots are made of plastic, but some growers still prefer to use the traditional clay pots even though they are more expensive. Plants growing in clay pots need more water than those in plastic pots, but provided watering and feeding are adjust-

When repotting a plant, the original soil ball should be level or just below the surface of the new soil

ed, the end results are similar. If you are planning to use capillary matting as an aid to watering, you must only use plastic pots because it is their inherent thinness that allows the compost to protrude through the drainage holes and touch the moist matting underneath.

Winterizing

The majority of fuchsias cannot withstand frost, so in cold areas they must be given winter protection. The best way to winter fuchsias is to keep them at a temperature close to 50°F (10°C), so they retain their leaves and continue to grow slowly. Watering and feeding must be kept to a minimum. Very few losses, if any, should be experienced. Plants that have been placed in the garden in tubs must be moved back into the greenhouse for the winter or they may die. Any tender cultivars that have been planted in beds will have to be dug up and put in pots. Large plants can be pruned back by cutting off approximately two-thirds of each stem. This not only helps to reduce the amount of space each takes up, but also removes unripe wood at the tip of the stems which is unlikely to survive the winter.

If your greenhouse is small and the size of the plants a problem, take cuttings in late summer. They will take up much less room than their parents, so a much larger number can be kept in the same space. The old plants can then be left outside to fend for themselves. Many will die but in mild areas a surprising number may survive. If particular cultivars continue to survive for many seasons they will sometimes be accepted as hardy garden plants.

Plants like the one shown below will need to be protected from frost or they are unlikely to survive. This means moving them into a heated greenhouse or conservatory for the winter

Unfortunately, heating a greenhouse to 50°F (10°C) can be expensive, so you may find it necessary to reduce the minimum temperature. Set the heating system at 42°F (5°C), rather than freezing point itself (32°F [0°C]), to have a margin for error. As winter sets in and this minimum temperature approaches, keep the plants dry at the roots but do not let them become dust-dry. At this point the leaves will begin to fall and the plants become dormant. They must not be allowed to become so dry that the stems begin to lose water or they may become permanently dormant – i.e., dead! The exact water requirement at this time can only be learned by personal experience, as it cannot be easily described.

Plants die through two main causes. Most commonly they become frost-damaged. Many heating systems may seem adequate during the daytime but prove completely inadequate on cold nights.

The answer is to use the best heating system you can afford; one controlled by a thermostat is almost essential, but regularly check its operation by using a maximum-minimum thermometer. Second, plants die by dehydration when kept too dry at the roots for too long. If you are certain that dead plants have not been frost-damaged, this is the most likely cause.

Unfortunately, even if you are doing everything right a few plants may still die. Nobody can guarantee complete success, but if a significant number of plants fail to survive, one or both of these causes is probably the culprit.

Even if you do not have a heated greenhouse it is still possible to winterize

fuchsia plants. The following method relies on the insulating power of peat to protect them from freezing. Keep the plants growing for as long as possible, but before the first frost remove them from their pots or dig them up if they are in the garden. All remaining leaves must be removed, and the top two-thirds of each stem pruned away using sharp pruning shears. If required, some or all of the soil can be shaken from the roots, but this is not essential.

The plants are then roughly bundled together and placed on the greenhouse floor, whether it is concrete or dry soil. Next they are covered with peat to a depth of at least 6 in. (15 cm). A covering of old sacks on top of the heap gives greater protection.

The peat should not be wet or bone-dry (if the former the plants rot, and if the latter they dehydrate and die). Test the peat by trying to squeeze water from it – if you can, it is too wet, and if no water is expelled but it stays together in a ball, it is still too wet. Throw a little peat into the air. If some of the fine particles float away in the wind, then it is too dry. But if this does not happen, and it can be poured over the plants without falling in large lumps, then it is just about right.

If the site is prone to winter flooding, raise the fuchsias clear of the ground, or place them on staging, but remember they also require a thick layer of peat underneath. Large specimens such as standards can also be treated in this way. This method of winterizing will not always work, and some losses are to be expected. On the other hand I know of growers who simply dig a hole in the ground outside and bury their plants for the winter. A surprising number survive.

The plants should be uncovered as soon as the weather begins to warm up in the spring, and be re-planted in the smallest-possible pots. They can be protected temporarily on cold nights by placing old newspapers over them. Treat plants normally once they start to grow.

If greenhouse space is restricted, plants brought in from outside may need to be pruned. The above illustration shows the plant on the opposite page after two-thirds of each stem has been cut away. Note that this has been done in a way that reshapes the plant for the start of growth next season

The choice of heating system is quite important as they vary in design. Those that burn fuel often vent directly into the greenhouse. It does not matter whether the fuel is kerosene or bottled gas because both, when burned, produce slightly more than their own weight of water. This makes the atmosphere very moist and encourages mold diseases. Sometimes kerosene heaters flare up and release soot and fumes into the greenhouse. This can be caused by a badly serviced heater, or more likely a lack of air. If you use this type of heater there must be a way for fresh air to enter the greenhouse. It may be necessary to leave one ventilator open slightly, not just to allow air to enter, but so that moist air can escape.

The more expensive heaters have a heat exchanger so that combustion gases are vented to the outside through a flue. Heaters that burn coal must have a flue as the combustion gases are poisonous. Note that the fumes created by burning domestic heating oil in a heater designed for kerosene will seriously damage your plants, because kerosene is more highly refined.

37

Electric heaters are relatively cheap and economical. Electricity and water are a dangerous combination, and the power supply to a greenhouse should be installed by a professional. Unfortunately, the cost of installation can be very expensive, but cutting corners here would be a false economy. Heating by electricity is generally considered the most convenient and efficient. It only takes the flick of a switch to operate the heater and a good thermostat ensures that heat is not wasted. Make sure that the model you buy has a separate thermostat, preferably of the rod type, rather than one built into the casing. The other big advantage of electrical heating is that it does not put water into the air so that a rise in temperature lowers the relative humidity. In winter this helps to prevent the formation of fungal diseases such as botrytis. Most electric greenhouses heaters contain a built-in fan which circulates the air and also helps to prevent disease. To conserve energy all heated greenhouses should have an insulating lining to prevent excessive heat loss. This can be accomplished by attaching sheets of transparent plastic film on the inside of the structure. Thin sheets of polyethylene can be attached to the inside of wooden structures with wooden battens, or large-headed tacks.

Metal houses can be lined in a similar manner by using small plastic clips in the grooves on the glazing bars. Remember that some air must be allowed to enter at all times, so do not make the structure airtight. In addition to plain plastic sheeting, bubble plastic, often used as a protective wrapping, can also be used.

Opposite: "Fuchsiade 88." This fine plant, originally introduced as a tender cultivar, has been shown to be very hardy and the plant depicted has survived for three years in the author's garden and is already blooming in early July

Below: "Mood Indigo" is a recent introduction from De Graaff in the Netherlands. The growth is strong, multi-branching and pendulous

Growing Fuchsias in the Garden

In the spring, after the last danger of frost, virtually all fuchsias can be planted outdoors. In Victorian England some flower beds were entirely planted with fuchsias, some for their flowers, and some for their colored foliage. Most will have to be lifted and returned to the heated greenhouse before the next frosts or they will die.

However, some will survive quite severe frosts and can be planted as permanent garden shrubs. In the coldest areas these plants will be killed back to ground level and new shoots appear from below the soil surface. But in milder areas, where severe frosts are rare, the aerial stems will survive and the plants get larger each year. In the milder parts of the west coast of Scotland, England, and Ireland, fuchsias have escaped from cultivation and are found growing wild in the hedgerows.

To stand a good chance of establishing fuchsias permanently in your garden, you must first choose a suitable cultivar (a list of recommended plants is given in on page 121). It is also important to plant hardy fuchsias in the right way, at the right time. Because new stems only grow from old ones and do not grow from roots, it is important not to plant too shallowly. The best method is

to prepare the soil by digging, incorporating manure, etc., and then plant each fuchsia in a saucer-like depression in the ground about 4 in. (10 cm) deep and about 12 in. (30 cm) across. The soil ball should be planted in a hole in the center, about 1 in. (2.5 cm) below the bottom of the depression. As the season develops, gradually fill in the depression so that the soil level is eventually flush with the surrounding soil. This should result in at least 4-5 in. (10-13 cm) of stem being buried below soil level. As an added precaution, the area of soil around the base of the plant can be covered with a layer of peat or

mulch before the onset of cold weather.

The best time to plant new hardy fuchsias is as soon as possible after the last frost. They will then have the summer months to grow and fully establish themselves before the first critical winter. Do not plant rooted cuttings directly in the open. Always grow them in pots until they are well-established in 5 in. (13 cm), or larger pots, as they will

This garden scene shows several standard trained fuchsia growing in large tubs or pots. They are ideal for brightening gardens in summer, particularly when surrounded by non-flowering subjects such as conifers

stand a much better chance of survival. Also remember that greenhouse-grown plants should be gradually hardened before consigning them to life in the garden.

Keep the plants well-watered at all times, and choose a position where they will receive at least a few hours of direct sunshine each day. The type of soil is not critical, but it should not waterlog in winter or dry out quickly in summer. Hedges are planted in a similar manner, allowing 24-48 in. (61-122 cm) between each plant, the exact distance depending on the cultivar used.

Fuchsias are one of the few flowering shrubs that do better in a wet summer than a dry one. In northwest Europe fuchsias established outside usually start to flower in July and continue until the first hard frost. In mild areas, where stems continue to grow from year to year, they will need pruning to

The reason why some fuchsias are hardier in the garden than others is not fully understood. Partly it is an inherited characteristic, because the species from which they were developed live naturally in a cold climate. However, constitutional factors such as vigor must also be involved. Some plants recover to form large free-flowering shrubs after complete destruction of their aerial stems in winter. Others survive frost but then fail to put out enough growth to make a satisfactory display for the following season.

"Tom Thumb" and its sports are interesting, as they are quite small and cannot be regarded as vigorous when compared with tall growing plants like "Riccartonii." Despite this apparent disadvantage they are some of the most hardy fuchsias available. The secret of their success seems to lie in the ability to form many underground stems, each with many potential growing points. During spring, so many stems emerge from belowground that the large number of leaves helps the plants to recover from winter damage.

prevent them from becoming too large. They will also become woody at the base if they are not cut back at the start of each season.

The amount of pruning can be as much or as little as you like. Well-established plants can be cut back to stumps with relatively little fear that they will die. In cold areas the stems will be largely pruned by nature, so it is only necessary to remove dead wood. This must be carried out in spring after the new growth has started, otherwise there is a danger that you will prune away live material. Do not cut the dead wood down to ground level but leave about 4-5 in. (10-13 cm) above the surface. This will help give support and protection to the new stems as they emerge. Treat hedges as individual bushes.

Above: Fuchsias that are planted out permanently in the garden should be planted in a shallow depression in the ground which is gradually filled in as the season progresses

Right: A collection of fuchsias stored in a greenhouse for the winter

Propagation

Many people have asked me when is the best time to take a cutting from a fuchsia. It is a difficult question to answer as the best time is not the same for everyone. If you visit someone's garden in late summer and marvel at a magnificent display of flowering fuchsias and are told that you can take cuttings, that is definitely the best time! But if you want to grow a plant to exhibit in next year's midsummer flower show, and the class is limited to a pot no larger than 4 in. (10 cm), you must propagate in very early spring, under heat. However, if the pot size is unlimited (and remember, a good big plant beats a

Right: "Brookwood Belle." This is one of the best red-and-white flowering cultivars for training as a bush or standard. Because it flowers so freely it is best propagated in the early spring before flower buds start to form

good small one), you need to propagate the previous year. There is no best time to propagate as it depends on individual need, circumstances, and the facilities available. A skilled fuchsia grower must be able to take cuttings at almost any time of year.

If the question were to be asked, "When is the easiest time to take cuttings?" the answer is clear – take them in spring, when new growth exceeds 1-2 in. (2.5-5 cm), and before flower buds start to form. The exact times will depend on where you live and the temperature in your greenhouse. If the plants have been wintered in a warm greenhouse this time could be as early as January, but if they have been wintered by plunging them in a bed of peat it could be as late as April.

Cuttings taken at this stage, without flower buds, are in a growing phase and root very easily, with few losses. Once flower buds start to form, cuttings root much more slowly and losses are greater.

Even if you have a greenhouse heated to 50°F (10°C) you may still have to delay rooting cuttings unless a propagator heated to a temperature of about 65°F (18°C) is available. To have the greatest success in rooting cuttings, some form of propagator is essential. Commercially made products can be inexpensive and are much safer to use.

Propagators need a means of heating and this must be accurately regu-

lated. Electrically powered models are a distinct advantage but must have an electricity supply installed in a greenhouse by a professional. Also, there must be a means of controlling humidity. This is usually achieved by use of a large transparent plastic cover which encloses the cuttings. There are many commercial designs in this basic pattern available and some large garden centers also stock electric heating cables for do-it-yourself models. They are buried in a 4 in. (10 cm) layer of washed sand contained in a

wooden surround. The top is covered by a plastic sheet, and the temperature inside controlled by a thermostat, preferably of the more accurate rod type. Sometimes these cables can be plugged directly into household current, but usually a transformer is required. The cables, thermostat, and transformer are designed especially for greenhouses and are normally supplied ready-wired, and are safe to use. If in doubt, consult a qualified electrician.

Opposite bottom: The illustration shows a heated propagation bench controlled by a rod thermostat. An irrigation nozzle can be seen that frequently mists over the cuttings with water to prevent them from wilting

Left: This propagator is controlled by a rod thermostat and water is supplied to capillary matting from the bowl at the left. Some cuttings have humidity increased around them by covering them with transparent plastic covers

Propagation from Spring Cuttings

This method uses the soft tip cuttings that emerge as new growth in early spring and before they show signs of flowering. The best cuttings come from plants that have been completely dormant in winter. Under normal conditions in northwest Europe, new shoots will start to appear on greenhouse plants in late February or March, depending on the temperature being maintained. As soon as the new shoots are 1-2 in. (2.5-5 cm) long they can be severed close to the mother plant with a sharp blade. These cuttings need very little preparation before being planted. Any leaves on the lower ½ in. (13 mm) must be removed. Since these cuttings do not need trimming below a leaf node, no further preparation is necessary. It is very important at this stage to prevent the cuttings from wilting. If this is a problem when the weather is hot, drop them into a container full of water until they are ready for planting.

Because these cuttings root readily it is not absolutely necessary to use a hormone rooting compound for success. However, some contain a fungicide which may help to prevent the cuttings from rotting if conditions are not perfect. I always recommend the use of these products.

Some hormone rooting powders are produced in a range of strengths, so try to select a product that is suitable for softwood cuttings. If you have plunged the cuttings into water to prevent them from wilting, dry the ends on absorbent paper before dipping them in the preparation. The cuttings are now ready for planting.

Left: Autumn cuttings are taken by removing a suitable shoot from the main stem with a downward tearing motion

The cuttings will root in many different rooting media such as perlite, sand, and vermiculite. However, these products do not contain any plant nutrients, so it is necessary to transplant the cuttings as soon as they have rooted, or they will suffer a serious check in growth. The best medium to use is a soilless compost specifically designed for sowing seeds and rooting cuttings. Do not use ordinary garden soil or potting compost. The former will contain many pests and diseases, and the fertilizer content of the latter will be too high, inhibiting the formation of roots.

The cuttings can be planted up to 40 together in a standard-size seed tray or, better still, planted in small individual pots or modules. Individually rooted cuttings suffer much less disturbance when they are transplanted than those grown in trays. Insert the cuttings approximately ½ in. (13 mm) deep in the compost and avoid tamping down.

As soon as all the cuttings have been planted, water them well and place them immediately in the propagator at a temperature of between 60-68°F (16-20°C). Ensure that any ventilator holes in the lid of the propagator are closed to create maximum humidity.

If you have only a small number of cuttings to root, they can be conveniently planted together in a small flower pot or separately in small pots contained in a tray. This can be covered in a clear plastic bag to retain moisture. It may be necessary to insert lengths of bent wire or small sticks into the pots to lift up the plastic, as it must not touch the cuttings. Provided you can maintain a steady temperature of near 64°F (18°C), the cuttings will root as well as in a commercial propagator.

Any propagator should be capable of maintaining the required minimum temperature reasonably accurately, but it cannot reduce the temperature if it rises above the maximum limit. This has to be done manually by shading. Do not remove the cover or the necessary humidity will be lost. No direct or even hazy sunlight should be allowed to fall on the newly planted cuttings or you will cook them. Remember how hot it is when you return to a car that has been left in the sun with the windows closed. Many growers leave their newly planted cuttings in a cool greenhouse in the early morning, go to work, and return in the cool of the evening to find them all dead – and wonder why?

During the rooting period the cuttings should be examined every day. If any signs of rot or gray mold appear, remove all infected leaves and slightly open the propagator's ventilation holes. After about 10 days, spring cuttings should be starting to root. The dull "pinched" look should give way to a brighter, more shiny one.

The ventilation holes in the propagator can now be fully opened, or the plastic film or bag loosened to let in fresh air. After a few more days the covering can be removed completely. However, if the weather suddenly

Right: A cutting ready for planting. Spring and summer cuttings are similar in appearance but a summer cutting, shown here, should be trimmed below a leaf node

Propagation from Summer Cuttings

After the burst of fresh spring growth, fuchsias start to form flower buds in early summer. Although the plant hormones are changing, making rooting more difficult, many growers have to take cuttings now. Not only is the quality of cuttings not so good, but it is more difficult to keep the propagator below the maximum recommended temperature of about 80°F (26°C). Heavy shading may be necessary, but this must not be overdone as it can also impair rooting.

The cuttings should be taken from the tips of the stems. If possible, select strong growth without any flower buds. The stems should be cut off with a sharp blade just above a node, and the cuttings trimmed to just below a node. This avoids leaving a "snag" or ugly piece of stem on the mother plant which might begin to rot if the air is cool and damp. The lower leaves and any flower buds should be carefully removed before planting.

The length of the cuttings should slightly exceed those taken in spring, measuring about 2-3 in. (5-7.5 cm) from tip to base. Note that these cuttings are trimmed to just below a leaf node because this is where the natural root-forming hormones are most concentrated. For best results also use a commercial hormone rooting preparation.

The cuttings are planted like spring cuttings, and treated in an identical manner. However, during the rooting period, even before the roots have formed, any remaining embryo flower buds will grow rapidly and should be removed when they become large enough to handle. Summer cuttings take up to two weeks to root, and final losses will exceed those taken in spring.

turns hot it may be necessary to replace the lid or bag temporarily to prevent excess wilting. Alternatively, the newly rooted cuttings can be lightly sprayed from time to time with clean water. As soon as the cuttings seem happy in the open air they can be moved into a slightly brighter position for a few days before being repotted or transplanted in a larger pot as described in the previous chapter.

In the vast majority of cases there is little difference in the ease of rooting between various cultivars, but occasionally, some such as "Texas Longhorn" can be more difficult. If you have problems rooting cuttings, the trouble may lie in their quality rather than a fault in the technique of rooting them.

The main characteristic that affects ease of rooting is the rate of growth of the mother plant at the time the cuttings are taken. Rapidly growing plants produce young and soft cuttings that root easily and quickly. Flowering plants, or those that are underwatered or underfed, give harder, more woody cuttings that root more slowly with greater losses.

Summer cuttings will often have flower buds which must be removed before planting. Note that the cutting has been taken just above a leaf node to avoid leaving a "snag" on the mother plant. The cutting should be trimmed to just below a node before insertion as shown on the opposite page

Propagation from Autumn Cuttings

These are best taken in late summer or early autumn, well before the first frost. The techniques are slightly different from those already described for spring and summer cuttings. Instead of cutting off the tips of branches, short side shoots are torn away from the main stems. Shoots about 4-6 in. (10-15 cm) long are ideal, and will be found a little way down from the tip of the main stem. As they are torn away from the mother plant they should retain a small "heel" of more mature wood from the main stem. This heel, if too long, should be trimmed.

The lower two pairs of leaves should also be removed and, after dipping in hormone rooting powder, the cuttings are inserted into compost to a depth of 1-2 in. (2.5-5 cm). Water well and treat as described for spring and summer cuttings. After about 14 days open the ventilator holes in the propagator even though the cuttings may not have rooted and, after a few more days, remove the lid completely. Very often these cuttings take a long time to root and frequently drop their leaves as winter approaches. If this happens keep them at around 50°F (10°C), and do not let the soil dry out completely. Although they do not have roots at this stage, do not be in a hurry to throw away apparent failures; the roots often form in the spring when the new leaves start to appear.

Opposite: This cutting clearly shows a "heel" at the end of the stem which is formed as the cutting is torn away from the main stem. The thinnest part at the tip of the heel should be cut away before the cuttings are planted

Right: "Leonora" is a single flowered cultivar that "sported" to give the double flowered "Hampshire Leonora" (shown on page 50)

Sports and Mutations

Sometimes something happens to an embryo bud to make it change its character. For example, the flowers may be a different color from the rest of the plant; or double-flowered instead of single and vice versa; or the foliage might even be variegated. The reasons why this happens are not fully understood. It may be caused by insect damage, though radiation and some naturally occurring chemicals such as colchicine can cause these mutations. Some laboratories deliberately attempt to produce such mutations, or sports as they are often called, for their commercial possibilities.

If you find a mutation that is worth keeping, prune away some of the normal stems to encourage it to grow more rapidly. When it is large enough, take a cutting and root as previously described (according to the time of year). In case of failure, keep the parent plant so that

Left:
"Cardinal Farges" is a red-and-white sport from "Abbé Farges" (see below)

Right:
"Hampshire Leonora" is a double-flowered sport from "Leonora"

Below:
"Abbé Farges"

more cuttings can be taken. The cuttings should retain the new characteristics but occasionally will wholly or partially revert to the normal form. If this happens, discard them. The new cultivar must be assessed by growing it for two or three years before you consider naming it.

This is where an important warning must be given. Mutations very frequently, if not always, happen more than once. Your beautiful new cultivar might not be new at all, and could have already occurred more than once in many parts of the world. "Heidi Weiss," "White Heidi Ann," and "White Ann" are all identical red-and-white flowered sports from the red-and-mauve flowered "Heidi Ann." It is also quite possible that your sport is not a new form, but merely a reversion to its original parent, an already well-known cultivar. Even if your new cultivar appears to be unique, the International Code of Nomenclature requires that it be named with reference to its progenitor. For example, "White Heidi Ann" is acceptable as a named sport from "Heidi Ann," but "Jim's Joy" is not, no matter how delighted Jim may have been to raise it.

Propagation from Seed

Seed can be saved from your own plants or can be bought from some nurseries. The seed is small, often less than 1/25 in. (1 mm) in length. Fill a shallow pan with a good quality soilless seed compost and water it lightly. Sow the seeds on the surface and barely cover them with a fine layer of compost, dusted over the seeds using a fine sieve. Place a sheet of glass over the seed pan and cover with paper to keep out the light. Place the pan in a propagator at 60-68°F (16-20°C) and the seedlings should start to emerge within 14 days.

As soon as they emerge, remove the paper, followed a few days later by the covering glass. However, do not expect all the seedlings to emerge; typical germination success rates are about 30 percent. As soon as the seedlings are large enough to handle, carefully hold them by their leaves and tease them from the compost, and pot them separately in small containers. Seed sown in early spring will result in plants that flower from midsummer onwards.

Seed purchased from commercial sources is usually described as mixed hybrids. It will have been obtained from selected mother plants which will have set seed naturally. Except in one or two special cases, pollination will not have been carried out by hand, so all the seedlings will be of unpredictable colors. Generally, they give a reasonable color range in both single and double flowers. There are very few named cultivars that can be grown from seed, and their performance is rather disappointing. Until further improvements have been made they are best avoided.

Seed can also be saved from your own plants. Bees will often cross-pollinate or even self-pollinate fuchsia flowers. The blooms fall as they fade, leaving behind the embryo fruits as small, green swellings. When they are fully grown they turn deep red or purple, although a few cultivars just turn yellowish-green. In the latter case softness is the best guide to their maturity. The ripe fruits are either carefully dissected or squashed as gently as possible onto absorbent paper. As the juice soaks away, the tiny seeds should be visible in the flesh. Pollination may not be perfect in cultivation, and many fruits may have to be opened to find just a few seeds. Pick them off the paper with the tip of a pointed knife and sow as soon as possible.

A commercial seed grower in the Canary Islands once told me that in that climate, fuchsia seed pods dry out when they are ripe, and seed is extracted by breaking up the fruits and blowing away the debris. In northwest Europe over-ripe fruits just rot; techniques need to be adapted to suit the prevailing conditions.

In the wild, seed obtained from species should always breed true. However, there may be an occasional change in flower color or other slight deviation in some of the seedlings. Botanists regard these minor alterations as varieties of that species. Wild hybrids are sometimes found, but these are extremely rare. In cultivation, where many different species from different areas are brought together and unless suitable precautions are taken, there is a distinct risk that cross-pollination will occur. Therefore seed saved from these plants cannot be relied on to breed true to the species they were harvested from. Cuttings, whether taken from a species, a variety of a species, or a cultivar, will always be exactly like their parents unless a rare mutation has occurred.

Hybridization

This is the only way, apart from deliberately causing mutations to occur, to produce new fuchsia cultivars. The basic principle is to transfer pollen from the flower of one cultivar to the stigma of a different one. You can transfer pollen from one species to another, from cultivar to cultivar, or a combination of the two. Although this will work for many cultivars, in some cases there may be incompatibility problems, particularly between species from different sections in the genus.

Before embarking on a program of hybridization decide what you want to accomplish, and select likely parents. For example, you may want to produce a plant that has orange-and-white striped blooms. Try crossing an orange-flowered cultivar such as "Orange Drops" with a striped flower such as the red-and-white blooming "Satellite." Although genetics is beyond the scope of this book, it is worth mentioning that the aim of the above cross may not succeed in the first generation. If the desired character is recessive it may be necessary to cross-pollinate two of the resulting seedlings together before it begins to show in the second-generation offspring. Even then, there is no guarantee of success.

When hybridizing, begin by choosing a mother plant. Although the cultivar should be selected with care it need not be one of your healthiest plants, but it should be disease-free. If it needs repotting and is slightly starved, so much the better. Plants need a regular supply of water, light, and nutrition. Seeds are more robust and can survive for centuries. Plants growing in adverse conditions seem to sense this and are quick to flower and seed. The best time to start is in late spring or early summer so that the fruits ripen before winter. Once the mother plant has been found, select a large bud that is about to open or has just begun to split. At this stage no insects will have been able to pollinate it (in any case the stigma and anthers will not have matured). Carefully open the bloom and, with a pair of scissors, cut away the anthers. This process of emasculation means that the pollen-producing parts cannot self-fertilize the bloom.

Repeat on several other flowers before covering each with a small muslin bag to exclude bees or other pollinating insects. At this stage the stigma is not receptive to pollen, but within a few days of emasculation, this will change; the exact timing is difficult to predict. The muslin bags should be removed each day and the stigma examined. When unripe, the lobes appear dull and dry, but as they mature they become sticky and slightly more shiny.

When the stigma is mature, pollen from the selected father plant is dusted onto it. Some people cut the anthers from the flowers and dab them directly onto the stigma, while others prefer to transfer the pollen with a clean camel-hair brush.

Afterwards, plenty of pollen grains should be seen adhering to the stigma. If the stigma is not ripe enough the pollen will not stick, and the procedure must be repeated the next day. In either case the muslin bags must be replaced or bees may transfer pollen from a number of other cultivars and ruin your plans. The stigma will start to die a few days after successful pollination, and the bags can be removed.

If everything has gone according to plan, marvelous things start to happen. The pollen germinates on the stigma and sends out an extension that grows through it, right down the style into the ovary. Considering how small a grain of pollen is, and that the journey to the ovary can often be 2 in. (5 cm), this is an amazing feat. The time taken for the fruit to ripen varies, but it is typically about 10 weeks from pollination. Most fuchsias have fruits that measure no larger than $\frac{2}{5}$ in. (15 mm) in length, although *F. procumbens*, a species from New Zealand, has fruits the size of small plums. The seeds can be extracted from the ripe fruits and sown as described on page 51.

Hybridization

Step 1. The selected bud is opened by hand to expose the immature sexual organs

Step 2. All the anthers, the parts that carry the pollen, are cut away with a pair of fine-pointed scissors. The emasculated flower is then covered in a muslin bag

Step 3. When the stigma has ripened, pollen is transferred to it from the selected father plant with the help of a camel-hair brush

Step 4. After fertilization, the flowers must be covered again with a muslin bag to prevent unwanted pollination by insects

Seedlings that show little or no improvement on their parents should not be named. They should also be well tested and grown for several years before release. Each cross can result in a very variable number of seedlings. Sometimes you struggle to produce just a few plants; in other cases you may get hundreds. Until they have been in flower for some time, and begin to show their full potential, you do not know if you have raised a winner.

In my own case I raise the seedlings until they are large enough to be planted outside in early summer in a test bed. In the autumn I select perhaps half a dozen of the most promising, and discard the rest. The selected plants are then grown and propagated under glass for at least two more years, before a final decision is made. This is how the fuchsia "Hampshire Treasure," a cross between "Lord Lonsdale" and "Bicentennial," was selected from 126 raised seedlings. If in doubt, contact a local specialty nursery, your local fuchsia society, or the American Fuchsia Society (at County Fair Building, 9th Avenue and Lincoln Way, San Francisco, California 94122, U.S.A.).

The ease of seed formation varies greatly between cultivars. Some set seed very easily without attention, but others need careful coaxing and hand-pollination to produce just a few. Unless they are needed, fruits should be removed from plants as they suppress flower formation. When fully ripe, the fruits fall and sometimes seedlings from them appear on or below the staging. By their survival in adverse conditions, these little plants show they are worth saving. Carefully dig up them up, pot them in small containers, and treat them as described above.

However, the most successful hybridists adopt a much more logical approach. Before trying to hybridize them, most will have already been growing fuchsias for many years. They will already have a number of favorite cultivars and have good ideas about the changes that need to be made to make them even better. Starting with these plants, crosses should be carried out and careful notes made of what has been done. After a number of years you may find that some plants are better at passing on the required character than others, so further crosses should be made using these plants or their seedlings.

The secret of successful hybridizing is to keep an accurate diary or "studbook" of all the crosses that are carried out so that in following years some sense can be made of the results. The majority of the most successful hybridists can tell you which plants they used and how many crosses it took to produce each of their cultivars.

Training and Exhibiting

Training is not essential. Fuchsias will grow and flower perfectly happily by themselves without being shown what to do. However, if you are going to produce standards, pillars, or fans, or want to win prizes at shows, read on. Training can be as simple as removing a few growing points, or might take years to grow a pyramid – the choice is yours.

Fuchsia cultivars vary greatly in their natural characteristics. Some are slow, almost weak growers. Others are extremely vigor-

Right: Standards are one of the most popular ways to train fuchsias. Table standards can be grown in one season, but taller specimens like the one shown here can take up to 18 months to grow

ous, and are best grown in greenhouse borders rather than pots. Stems vary in substance and strength. For example, "Preston Guild" always produces stiff, uncompromisingly upright stems, while "Autumnale" and "Orange Flare" produce strong, stiff stems that almost grow almost horizontally. The beautiful "Sophisticated Lady" and "Pink

Marshmallow" have stems that hang down like wet string. "Preston Guild" is a poor choice for a hanging basket but might look fine in the center of an urn or tub. Other cultivars have a gradation of characteristics between these extremes. Before you start to train a plant you need to know its merits and limitations for a particular purpose. See the list of recommended cultivars on page 120.

The Bush Form

The bush is the simplest shape for training a fuchsia, and is also the starting point for producing more exotic forms. Beginners should start by growing a bush before attempting anything more complicated. Choose a cultivar that has naturally upright or stiff stems. Remember that some cultivars, such as "Hampshire Prince," have stems that grow upright at first but later trail down under the weight of the huge blooms. Others, such as "Nellie Nuttall" and "Marilyn Olsen," are naturally free-branching and need little training, while those such as "Texas Longhorn" require considerable work if they are to look attractive.

Bush training starts at a very early stage and should commence as soon as a rooted cutting has been potted and grown about four pairs of leaves. The growing tip is cut out using a sharp blade, or pinched out with the fingernails (known as stopping). This results in the plant's energy being channeled into the remaining growing points, the side shoots. Young cuttings that are growing as a single stem produce branches from the leaf joints, and existing branches will quickly lengthen.

As soon as the side branches produce four pairs of leaves they should again be stopped by removing the growing tips. Repeating the process once more is all that is necessary to form a good, decorative bush. However, exhibitors often stop their plants at every two or three pairs of leaves, and carry on the process for as long as possible until the flower buds must be allowed to develop.

As the plants grow it may be necessary to insert small canes among the stems to provide some support. Eventually flower buds will develop at the tip of each stem; the more stems that form, the more flowers will be produced. However, since stopping also delays flowering you must reach a compromise between improving the shape of the plant and the time of flowering. If the aim is to grow a plant for general purposes, pinching the growing tips on three separate occasions usually gives fine results.

Below: After potting, all the growing tips are then pinched out using the fingernails or a sharp blade

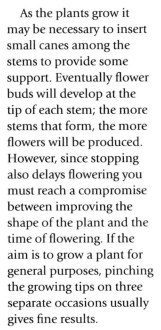

Left: The illustration shows a cutting that has been potted and is now established. Training into a bush starts at this point when three to four pairs of leaves have been formed

Right: When the side shoots have grown three or four more pairs of leaves they are again "stopped" by pinching out the growing tips

Hanging Baskets

Hanging baskets are only a specialized form of the bush fuchsia described on page 56. The aim of a hanging basket is to produce a large cascade of blooms that completely hides the container. For this reason pendant cultivars are usually chosen. Unlike bush fuchsias that can be repotted as often as needed, hanging baskets are planted only once to last a complete season or more. For this reason a basket measuring at least 16 in. (41 cm) in diameter should be chosen. Also select one that has reasonable depth so that a good volume of compost can be used. Commercially, hanging baskets are made of wire or plastic. Depending on which type is used, they have to be planted in different ways.

To plant a hanging basket you will need some sort of liner, three or five well-rooted cuttings, and some good-quality potting compost

Traditional hanging baskets are made of wire that has been galvanized, or plastic-coated for durability. They must be lined to prevent the compost from falling through the holes. Traditionally, live sphagnum moss is used, but alternatives include plastic sheeting and special liners available from garden centers. They can look unattractive until the plants grow large enough to hide them completely.

To line and fill a basket, first stand it on a pan or half-pot so that it does not roll around, and press the moss evenly over the inside. Make sure that a good top edge is formed; otherwise soil will be easily washed out when the basket is watered. Altern-

atively, place the plastic sheeting or liner neatly over the inside. Add good-quality potting compost until it is 1 in. (2.5 cm) below the top of the basket lining. The basket is then ready for planting.

Hanging baskets planted in this way dry out very quickly in hot weather, and sometimes need watering several times a day. To alleviate the problem you can line the inside of the moss with

57

plastic sheeting to help prevent evaporation. When using this technique, make several holes in the sheeting near the bottom of the basket so that water can drain away, or it may become waterlogged in wet weather. Alternatively, there are special resins that can be mixed with the compost to greatly improve its water-holding capacity without causing waterlogging.

Many people prefer to use a soil-based compost for hanging baskets because it has a longer life than the soilless kind, and is more manageable. However, one disadvantage of soil is that it makes the basket very heavy and therefore more difficult to hang up securely. If you decide to use a soilless compost instead, make sure that it contains a slow-release fertilizer as it will save a lot of time and maintenance later on.

Plant either three or five plants per basket, the exact number depending on the basket size and the vigor of your chosen cultivars. Either place three around the edge, or plant one in the center and four around the edge. I always recommend using only one culti-

Right: To fill a hanging basket you will need either three plants around the edge or one in the center with four around the edge. The choice depends on the size of basket and the cuttings

Below: The photograph shows a hanging basket that has just been planted up. The tips of all the stems should be pinched out to encourage side branches to form

var per basket. If you mix different cultivars they never look right because some always grow larger than others, giving the finished basket an unsymmetrical look.

Hanging baskets are usually planted in the spring under glass, and placed outside in bloom after the last of the frost. Immediately after planting all the tips of the main stems should be pinched out, as described on page 56. Doing this once or twice is usually sufficient because the number of plants in each basket soon creates enough stems for a good display. No other maintenance is needed

except that hanging baskets need a great deal of watering and regular feeding, particularly if the basket is on the small side.

Plastic baskets are an alternative, and do not need lining, but most are rather too small and shallow, and cannot hold sufficient compost. However, if you can find one large enough, it should be easier to maintain than a wire basket because it will need less-frequent watering.

Some growers train cultivars with semi-stiff stems in baskets by hanging weights on their branches to encourage them to droop. This is unnecessary as there are so many naturally trailing cultivars to choose from.

Standards

This is where many beginners want to start and where many become disillusioned or disappointed. A standard is only a bush growing on a long stem, so when the art of growing a bush has been mastered, a good standard will follow.

Not all cultivars are equally easy to grow as standards; in fact some are very difficult (see page 120 for a list of recommended cultivars). It is worthwhile to take a special batch of cuttings for growing as standards or, when you are buying young plants, tell the nursery clerk what you want them for. Take the cuttings in the normal way, as early as you can in the year.

If you carefully look at fuchsias you will find that some cultivars occasionally produce a stem that has leaves in sets of three, instead of pairs. Use the former for growing standards. At the base of each leaf is a potential point of growth, and it is easier to form a bushy head by starting with three branches than two. If you cannot find cuttings of this sort do not worry; it is a minor point and very good results can be obtained with either type.

Standard fuchsia "whips" should be grown up a stake and tied to it at intervals of approximately 2 in. (5 cm)

Always take many more cuttings than you think you need; six for every standard required is not excessive. Choose only the strongest to develop and discard the rest. When rooted, the cuttings should be repotted in larger pots and a small cane placed close to each plant for support. As the cuttings grow they should be loosely tied to the cane at intervals of about every 2 in. (5 cm), so that the stems are kept as straight as possible. All the side shoots should be removed when they are large enough to handle, but you must retain the leaves on the main stem.

The side shoots can be cut away with a sharp blade, or torn away by holding them between thumb and finger, and pulling sideways.

After a few weeks you will almost certainly notice that some of the young standards are more vigorous than others; these are the ones to retain. If you are tough enough you can throw away the weak ones, or better still give them to your competitors at the gardening club. Remember that standard fuchsias take up a great deal of space and must be kept frost-free in winter.

At this stage, while the young fuchsias are being trained up a cane, and before they have started to form a head, they are known as "whips." While the whip is growing its growth must not be hindered, so it should be watered freely and repotted as necessary. It will also be periodically necessary to change the small supporting cane for a larger one, and to remove all side shoots as they form.

The ultimate height of the standard is a matter of preference. The British Fuchsia Society recognizes table standards as measuring 10-17 in. (25-43 cm) from the top of the compost to the lower branches of the head. Half-standards measure 18-29 in. (46-74 cm), and full standards 30-42 in. (76 cm-107cm). If you are not going to exhibit, you need not be governed by these rules.

When the whip has reached the desired height, pinch out the growing tip and retain the side shoots from the top three to five sets of leaves. These side shoots are the nucleus of the head, and when each has produced four pairs of leaves it should be stopped. The technique is now the same as for growing a bush. Keep all the leaves on the main stem for as long as possible, and try to retain them until the head has reached a substantial size. The stems forming the head are under considerable strain, even more so when in full bloom. To avoid whole

branches tearing themselves off under the weight you must give them some support.

Unlike bush-trained plants you cannot insert a few canes in the compost, but you can use lengths of thin garden twine to tie each major branch to the large supporting cane. For this reason the cane must extend right up through the head of the standard. Even if the cultivar being grown is one of the few that doesn't need extra support, the cane must still extend right into the head. If it does not there is a very real danger that the head will snap off from the main stem, at the topmost tie.

Standards need to be grown from cultivars that

naturally have reasonably stiff stems so that the head can be partly self-supporting. Very pendant cultivars, suitable for hanging baskets, pose no problem when being trained up a stake as a whip, but the branches of the head can droop in a mop-like, shapeless manner. However, there is a solution. Instead of using a bamboo cane as a support, substitute a 1 in. (2.5 cm) square wooden stake. At the top of the stake use a couple of strong staples to attach an inverted wire hanging basket, minus the chains. This makes an umbrella shape.

The head is then formed at the top part of the basket, and the stems are allowed to trail down over its surface. The stems can be neatly spaced over the

Above: Side shoots should be removed from the standard whips by tearing them away with a sideways movement

Right: When the standard has reached the required height, the tip of the main stem is pinched out with the fingernails or with a sharp blade. The top three to five sets of side shoots are left in place to form the head

basket by fastening them with small wire plant rings, or by tying with twine. The basket will eventually be hidden by the foliage and flowers, and a very attractive weeping standard is formed.

Fuchsia stems are very brittle and liable to break off if they are not well supported, but standards grown over hanging baskets are more robust. They are therefore more suitable for placing outdoors in summer, and are much less likely to be damaged by storms or accidents than those grown in the conventional way.

It is necessary to start growing standards early in

the year so that part of the head is formed by the next winter. Although a whip can be winterized, a noticeable kink develops in the stem when growth restarts in the spring. The only alternative is to maintain a minimum temperature of at least 50°F (10°C) during the winter so that growth does not stop. Some books say that if flowers start to develop while the whip is growing the standard will be useless.

Certainly you must avoid any check to growth and repot regularly, but as previously explained, the flowering cycle is controlled by hormones produced within the plants, which themselves are mainly controlled by day length. It is therefore virtually impossible to prevent whips or young standards from producing blooms during the summer. I have never managed to grow a standard without unwanted flower buds forming, so I do not believe this advice. I pick off any buds as soon as they are large enough to handle, just like the side shoots.

I have indicated that side shoots should be removed from the whip as soon as they are big enough to handle. There is an alternative school of thought that believes that they should all be allowed to develop four pairs of leaves and then be stopped. Only when the

head is well developed are the side shoots removed by cutting them away. The logic behind this is as follows. The green coloring matter in leaves is responsible for taking energy from sunlight and minerals from the roots and turning them into food the plants can use. The bigger the area of leaves the more food can be produced. By keeping only the leaves that grow on the main stem you may limit the rate of growth. If you want to grow a standard from an inherently weak or slow-growing cultivar it might be worth trying this method. On the other hand, I have grown standards up to 8 ft. (2.5 m) in height without problems by removing all side shoots as they form.

Pyramids

They are quite a challenge and only an expert fuchsia grower is likely to succeed. The ideal pyramid should be triangular in outline, rather like a Christmas tree. Pyramids take a lot of work and a lot of space in the greenhouse.

Only strong-growing, upright cultivars should be used, and you will need the strongest cuttings. Pot a cutting and insert a strong central cane to support the main stem, which should be tied to it at frequent intervals. When the main stem has grown

about 8 in. (20 cm) high, the growing tip should be removed. At this point the side shoots will develop strongly. When they have grown from four to six pairs of leaves the growing tips are removed, and only the two longest side shoots are left to develop.

The strongest, no matter where it comes from on the plant, should be tied to

Fan training begins by tying stems to vertical canes so that they grow in a flat plane. Afterwards, horizontal canes must be added to support the lateral branches

the stake to act as a new leader or main stem. This process temporarily diverts the plant's energy into the extending side shoots, which then grow longer than normal. If the lowest branches droop they will not develop properly, so they should be tied to canes inserted at an angle of about 45 degrees in the compost. This is only a temporary measure, and the supports can be removed when the pyramid is almost fully grown. The process of continued pinching-out of the growing is the way the broad triangular outline of the plant is achieved.

Fans and Espaliers

Basically, fans and espaliers are the same. The key difference is that fans are small espaliers grown on a framework of canes inserted into a pot, and espaliers are grown in a larger pot or bed, and are trained up a system of wires attached to the side of the greenhouse, or up a wall. This form of training is not often seen, but the method is quite simple. Cultivars that make good standards are equally suitable for growing as fans or espaliers.

To grow a fan, start with a strong-rooted cutting, pot it but do not pinch out the growing points. If you have not grown a fan before I recommend you start with "Peppermint Stick," as it has just the right characteristics. If everything goes according to plan you should end up with a rounded plant with a vertical center stem and well-developed side branches. At this stage cut away complete branches so that you are left with a flat fan shape. Try to keep the strongest branches and only remove the weakest. Support and spread the branches on canes placed in the pot, with cross-pieces to form a trellis. Repot as necessary, and replace the canes with

The early stages for training a fan is to tie the stems to a simple framework of canes and cut away any that grow at the wrong angle

larger ones as needed.

Espaliers are grown in a similar manner, but must be transferred to large pots as soon as development permits. The containers will need to be at least 8 in. (20 cm) diameter, and preferably about 10 in. (25 cm). The canes are removed and the branches spread out, fan-like, and tied to horizontal wires fixed at 6 in. (15 cm) intervals. If any side shoots from the main branches coincide with the horizontal wires, they should be trained along them. Those growing between the wires should be removed. When the leading stems have grown as long as required, pinch

out all their tips and the tips of the lateral growths. At this stage the plants can be allowed to flower.

At the end of the growing season, clean up the plants by removing any remaining flowers and dead leaves, and protect from the frost. In spring, prune back all lateral stems to about two leaf joints, remove from the supporting wires, and repot the plants with fresh compost. Re-tie all the stems to the framework and, as growth restarts, select one shoot from each lateral branch to replace the growth that has been pruned away.

63

Pillars

Pillars can be regarded as standards with the side shoots left on. They are shaped like tall cylinders and ideally should not taper from top to bottom.

The easiest way to grow one is to pot a strong cutting, insert a single cane for support, and allow the plant to develop. When the side shoots have produced four pairs of leaves, pinch them out, but leave the growing tip of the main stem to develop. From then on tie the central stem to the cane every 2 in. (5 cm), and trim the length of the side shoots as necessary to form a cylindrical shape. The lower branches will need quite severe pruning to control them. The plant must not suffer any setback, so it must be repotted and the cane replaced as necessary.

While this is a quick and easy method, it will invariably produce a shape wider at the bottom than the top. Another more complicated method gives better results. Start as before with a strong cutting, pot it, and insert a cane for support. Tie the main stem to the support every 2 in. (5 cm). When the cutting has grown four pairs of leaves the growing tip of the main stem is pinched out. After growing for a week or two, the two strongest side shoots are selected and all the others cut away where they join the main stem.

One of these shoots will be used to form the lower half of the plant, and the other the top half. I will refer to them as shoot (a) for the bottom half, and shoot (b) for the top half, and assume you want to grow a pillar 6½ ft. (2 m) tall. Shoot (a) is allowed to grow with its side shoots intact until it is 42 in. (100 cm) tall, when the growing tip is pinched out. It should be tied to the supporting stake at regular intervals. At the same time as shoot (a) is being trained, shoot (b) is tied to the same stake. Its side shoots are removed when they are large enough to handle, and the main growing point is left intact. Once (b) has grown to 42 in. (100 cm), all the side shoots are allowed to remain up to the full height of the pillar, when the growing tip is pinched out.

All the side shoots on both (a) and (b) are now trimmed to about 6 in. (15 cm) in length, making a cylinder about 12 in. (30 cm) wide from top to bottom. Short growths now appear from all the side shoots that will, when in flower, produce a cylindrical plant about 18 in. (46 cm) in diameter. Repot regularly because any check in growth will spoil the appearance of the finished plant. Getting good results from this method does need a considerable amount of experience and skill on the part of the grower.

Opposite: The magnificent pillar shown here is just about to burst into bloom

Right: A short pillar can be easily grown by training a cutting up a supporting cane and allowing the side shoots to develop. As the branches extend they should have the growing points pinched out when each one is about 9in. (23cm) In length so that the plant forms a cylinder about 18in. (46cm) in diameter

Exhibiting

My advice to the potential exhibitor and show winner is not to start by clearing a space to hold all the cups and medals you plan to win, but to read this chapter again. Most of what you need to know about growing prize-winning fuchsias is given in the above sections. The second most important tip is to obtain a show schedule well in advance. One from the previous year will be a lot better than nothing at all.

There is no point in entering a magnificent plant in a huge pot if the maximum container size is 6 in. (15 cm), or you will find your exhibit marked NAS (not according to schedule) by the judges. You must also be careful when entering plants in the hardy section. You can only enter plants that the show managers or society think are hardy, not necessarily those that you or your local nursery think are hardy. You can obtain a list of acceptable hardy cultivars from the show secretary.

Standard fuchsias and pelargoniums in one of the author's greenhouses in late spring

Timing is another critical factor. You need a superb display of blooms on the day itself, not before or after. Only trial and error under your own conditions will give you the best results, but as a rough guide allow 10-12 weeks from the last pinch for single-flowered cultivars, and 12-14 weeks for double-flowered types. I must emphasize that this advice can only be very approximate. It will vary at different times of the year, according to local conditions, and depend on whether the plants were showing embryo flower buds at the last pinch.

If your show plants look as if they are going to flower too late, there is little you can do to force them. If the weather is unseasonably cold you could turn on the heating system, but be careful not to dry out the atmosphere too much. Plants that are too advanced are much easier to deal with. Early flower buds can be picked off as soon as they are large enough to handle, and this can be continued for up to four weeks before the show. This should provide enough time for the small remaining buds to develop fully.

In fact, bringing the plants on early can be quite a good idea. Plants seem to sense that their flowers are not reaching maturity and react to disbudding by increasing the formation of buds. This ultimately leads to a temporary, but improved display on show day.

You must also know how judges award points, and what they are looking for. The rules vary from society to society, and from country to country, but there are points that are common to most. General appearance is important; yellowing leaves or leaves with holes must be removed. Pots should be clean, and all canes and ties well hidden among the foliage.

The plants must be named, and the name must be correct. Plants should be symmetrical and nicely rounded, and if more than one plant is required for a particular class they should be of similar shape and size.

A good judge will also know whether the plant is typical of the cultivar or species. For instance, a plant of "Waveney Gem" or "Marilyn Olsen" should be absolutely smothered in bloom, which is not always possible with "Garden Week" because it produces fewer but larger flowers. My advice is to grow only those that bloom very freely because not all judges know the difference.

Another problem that can occur is caused by the variability of flowers. Single flowers only have a corolla consisting of four petals. They are classed as semi-double if they have five to eight petals, and double if they have nine or more. Unfortunately many fuchsias do not understand the rules and occasionally grow a few extra petals. This can mean that if you enter a plant like this in the single-flowered section it will be disqualified. The descriptions in books and catalogs cannot always be relied on.

When the cultivar "Mieke Meursing" was introduced it was a sensation – the perfect show plant which produced masses of single pink blooms. It won many prizes at most shows. However, a few years later some growers found to their horror that their magnificent plants were being disqualified by judges because the blooms were now semi-double. All semi-double flowers are normally accepted as full doubles for show purposes, and should be entered in this class.

Before taking cuttings it is important to select good strong mother plants that produce the maximum number of blooms. Growers had obviously been selecting plants very carefully for this purpose, but apparently as a side effect, had also selected plants that had a tendency towards doubleness. This trend must have gradually increased over the years until it became noticed by judges.

Although the cultivar "Mieke Meursing" has been used here as an example, there are many other cultivars that can be used for exhibiting. Most of them have small- or medium-sized flowers and are naturally very bushy. This type of fuchsia seems to have the quality necessary to impress judges, and look superior to those with larger but fewer blooms.

Show plants are also subject to fashion. If one grower uses a new cultivar or rediscovers an old one, and wins the Best Plant in Show or other major award, you may be sure that it will be seen regularly at shows the following year. Visit a major flower show to see what is being currently used to win the prizes.

Part of one of the gold-medal winning displays grown and staged by the author at the Royal Horticultural Society's Chelsea Flower Show in London

Pests and Diseases

Well-grown fuchsias are not troubled by many pests or diseases. However, like all plants, they have their Achilles heel and are susceptible to a few problems that crop up fairly regularly. The main troubles are attacks by whitefly and aphids, and fuchsia rust.

Keeping a greenhouse or garden neat and tidy is not enough. Cleanliness is also vital. But how many gardeners wash their hands after touching a sick plant? If you want to stop an infectious disease, such as fuchsia rust, from spread-

ing, this is what you must do. Any parts of a plant that are removed, for whatever reason, should be placed in a plastic bag and consigned to the trash bin, not just dropped on the floor. Some say that all plant material should be burned, and it is certainly a good way of destroying diseased clippings, but it also pollutes the air and is illegal in many areas.

Weeds often carry pests and diseases. There is no point in keeping plants scrupulously clean if weeds under the greenhouse benches are constantly re-infecting them. Frequent checks should be made of all plants to remove dying leaves, and to check against the first signs of pests and diseases. The earlier you act, the easier problems are to eliminate. Once a disease has become well established it is much more difficult to cure, and is more likely to reoccur the following season.

Pests and diseases are spread in a number of ways. Sometimes infections are carried on the furry bodies of moths or are spread indirectly by scavenging insects. There is also the strong possibility that fuchsia rust is carried by human visitors on their clothing. To prevent infection I do not allow visitors to enter my main stock plant and propagation houses; even Ministry of Agriculture inspectors are asked to change into clean coats before entering the premises.

Once pests and diseases strike, there are two main ways of treating them. The first involves chemical control, and the second introducing a predator (either a creature or fungus) to feed on the pest. Both systems work and can sometimes be used together. However, while the chemical method can frequently eliminate pests, biological methods rely on a supply of the pest for the existence of the predator so complete control is rarely, if ever, achieved. It just reduces the level of attack to an acceptable level. The predators also predate on a

specific species, and a different one must be used for each pest. Chemical treatments often have a wider spectrum of activity and control many different pests with a single application. However, the trend is now toward chemicals with a specific action that will not harm beneficial insects, such as bees or biological predators.

Chemical treatments come in a range of formulations. For example, permethrin can be purchased as a spray or fog generator. The latter, often in the shape of a pellet or small firework, must be used in a tightly closed greenhouse so that the insecticidal mist permeates every nook and cranny. Fogs are quick and efficient, although relatively expensive, and not all chemicals can be used in this way.

Garden centers sell a wide range of garden chemicals. When used as directed they are very safe because they have passed stringent safety tests. Many growers do not appreciate that plants, not chemicals, are the most dangerous items in the garden. Generally, most plants do not want to be eaten so they have evolved powerful poisons to act as a deterrent to grazing animals. However, there is no known risk relating to fuchsias.

Biological control agents can be ordered from many garden centers or directly from a specialty supplier. One introduction of a parasite is not usually enough, and regular applications may be needed during the growing season.

Parasites are mainly used in the confined space of a greenhouse, but some can be used outdoors.

Proprietary names for chemicals and fungicides vary from country to country, and exactly the same active ingredients are often sold under different names by different manufacturers. For this reason, in the following sections, only the names of the active ingredients are given. They will be listed on the product's label. You must also read the small print because sometimes you will see that there are exclusions on the label such as "do not treat ferns, begonias, or fuchsias." Obviously, in these circumstances the manufacturers would not be held liable for damage to your plants. Fuchsias are sensitive to many garden chemicals. You should use chemicals in the evening, as an application in direct sunlight can cause scorching. There will also be fewer pollinating insects around at that time.

Finally, note that the availability of chemicals does vary, and that many old favorites are now being discontinued, while new ones are being introduced. Similarly, new predators for biological control are being regularly added to the list.

In addition to the pests listed on these pages you need to keep a careful watch for creatures that are not normally pests of fuchsias. The tube of this flower has been eaten by a mouse so that it could reach the sweet nectar at the base of the ovary

Pests

Aphids
(Greenfly, blackfly)

These insects suck the sap from young stems and leaves, causing considerable damage and distortion. They also secrete sugary honeydew which covers the leaves with a sticky deposit, and spread virus diseases. The predator *Aphidoletes aphidimyza* is a type of gall midge that lays its eggs next to aphid colonies, and the emerging larvae feed on the pest. The parasitic wasp *Aphidus colemani* and the fungus *Verticillium lecanii* can also be used. Alternatively, try chemical control using insecticides containing pirimicarb, permethrin or other pyrethrins, malathion or pirimiphos-methyl. Some manufacturers market specialized products called aphid or greenfly killers that contain one or more of these active ingredients.

The underside of this leaf shows the scales which are one of the whitefly's juvenile stages. The black scales show that these have been successfully attacked by the parasite *Encarsia formosa*

Capsid Bugs

These are yellowish-green insects that look like large slender aphids. The insects suck sap from the plants in the spring and early summer, and make holes in the leaves. They inject a poison in their saliva which causes the leaves to distort, and sometimes the growing points become blind and do not develop. The insects mainly affect outdoor plants, and sprays containing fenitrothion will give protection.

Caterpillars

The caterpillars of the elephant hawk moth, *Deilephila elpenor*, love fuchsias. If one finds its way onto your plants it can strip even a large one of most of its leaves. When fully grown the caterpillar is easily 3 in. (7.5 cm) long, and is not hard to find and identify. The moth is rather unusual and beautiful, so if you can sacrifice an occasional plant, so much the better. Otherwise, picking them off by hand is the best method of control. What you do with them is up to you; the obvious solution may not appeal to the squeamish. Caterpillars can also be controlled by sprays containing permethrin.

Cuckoo Spit
(Froghopper)

This is a small insect which signals its presence with a white froth which it secretes to cover itself. It feeds on the young shoots and leaves, and is normally only found on outdoor plants in the spring or early summer. The best means of control is to spray the plants with water to remove the protective spit, and then spray with an insecticide containing permethrin, pirimiphos-methyl, or malathion.

Red Spider Mite

This is a serious pest that spreads very quickly, especially in hot dry weather, and can do a lot of damage. The mites are virtually invisible to the naked eye but are detected by a dull brownish color that appears on the undersides of the leaves. The plants soon look lifeless and stunted, and the leaves start to fall in large numbers. In severe cases a fine web is evident under the leaves and over the tips of the shoots. As the pest is resistant to some chemicals, you may need to use

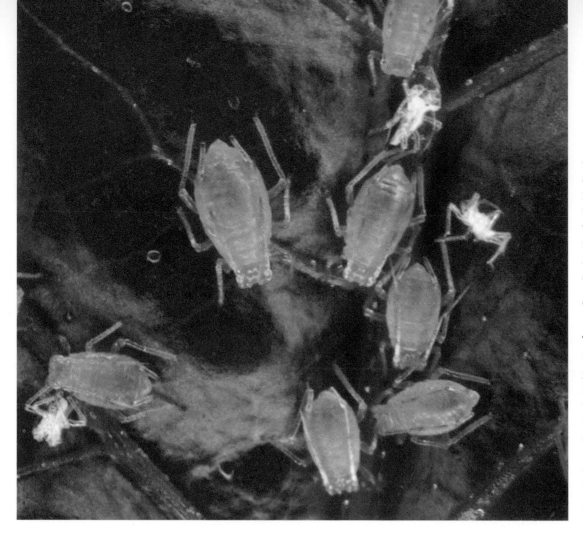

the predator *Phytoseiulus persimilis* in the greenhouse.

If you suspect this pest, order the parasite immediately because the parasites cannot control an established outbreak. If you get this pernicious pest one year it will almost certainly reoccur the next season as well, so introduce the parasite early next spring as a precaution. However, it is still worth trying sprays containing pirimiphos-methyl or bifenthrin.

Sciarid Flies
These are tiny gnat-like flies that breed in damp soil and are particularly fond of peat-based composts. They usually attack small seedlings only, and cause no noticeable damage to adult plants. However, recent research shows that these flies carry root-rot diseases from one source to another, and may cause the occasional, apparently inexplicable death of apparently unknown cause that seems to affect all types of plant from time to time. The parasitic nematodes *Heterorhabditus megadis* and *Steinernema carpocapsae* will control sciarid flies, or the surface of the soil can be dusted with a powder containing lindane.

Aphids, sometimes called greenfly or blackfly, commonly attack the young tips of fuchsias. They must be controlled as they damage the leaves and spread virus diseases

Vine Weevil
The adult beetle lays eggs in the soil in late summer and autumn, which hatch and eat the roots. The damage is most noticeable in spring when, here and there, the plants start to wilt badly. The grubs are fat and whitish, with brown heads. It is highly unlikely that the beetles walk into the greenhouse and climb the bench legs in order to lay their eggs in pots when they probably pass hundreds of other suitable sites on the way. The female adults are said to be unable to fly! Instead, it is most likely that vine weevils occurring in the greenhouse have been carried in by the grower in pots or plants

that have stood outside over summer. The best form of treatment is to water the soil with a culture of parasitic nematode worms, *Heterorhabditus megadis* or *Steinernema carpocapsae*.

Whitefly (*Trialeurodes vaporariorum*)
This is undoubtedly the most common pest of greenhouse fuchsias, and it can ruin a collection unless controlled. The adult insect resembles a small white moth which makes short flights when disturbed. It lays its eggs on the undersides of leaves and, although invisible to the naked eye, they soon hatch. The larvae are like small glassy scales.

Unfortunately, whitefly is resistant to many garden chemicals. Sprays containing bifenthrin, permethrin or pirimiphos-methyl are worth trying as some colonies are still susceptible to these chemicals, but they only kill the adults. Treatment has to be repeated frequently to kill the new adults as they emerge from the juvenile phases.

The parasitic wasp *Encarsia formosa* can be used in the greenhouse to control this pest, but it only attacks the larvae which turn black when infected. The wasp will not control an existing outbreak, so the need for treatment has to be anticipated and the parasite introduced at a very early stage. At best the pest is kept at tolerable levels. The greenhouse temperature must also be kept to at least 55°F (13°C) for the predator wasps to breed.

Although whiteflies are difficult to control there is hope for the future. Products like DDT have rightly earned the agrochemical industry a bad name. However, lessons have been learned and modern insecticides are efficient and very safe to use. Unfortunately, many people are now reluctant to use chemical methods of control for reasons that are completely out of date. New chemicals are now available to commercial growers that work like a miracle, but due to the high cost of registration they may not be released to the small amateur market that is still prepared to use chemicals. The young whiteflies go through several physical changes before they become adults. The new chemicals inhibit these changes, preventing insects from reaching adulthood and breeding. Mammals do not go through this process so the insecticide is virtually nonpoisonous to humans. It is also harmless to many other species including *Encarsia formosa*, the parasitic wasp.

Physiological Disorders

They are not actually diseases but are caused by faulty cultivation. The problem might be starvation, which can be cured by feeding, or leaf-color changes that are almost impossible to diagnose. Large brown patches on the upperside of leaves and stems are usually sunburns; shading is the remedy. If a nutritional problem is suspected, repotting is the best solution. Feeding might help, but this will not cure problems that are caused by the wrong pH (acidity or alkalinity) of the soil.

Some cultivars, especially the deep-purple flowered ones, seem to produce leaves that become multi-colored in shades of yellow, purple, and green. Repotting usually cures this problem, but some old leaves do this naturally as they come to the end of their lives. A certain amount of leaf drop is normal throughout the year.

Premature bud and leaf drop is usually caused by dryness, either at the roots or more likely in the atmosphere. Moving a plant from the greenhouse to the dry atmosphere of the house is frequently the cause. See also the entry on red spider mites.

Diseases

Fuchsia Rust (*Pucciniastrum epilobii*)
This fungus is characterized by slightly raised, orange blotches on the undersides of the leaves. If left untreated the leaves drop and the plant is weakened. The spores are highly contagious and can be spread by the wind. They are also spread on clothing and unwashed hands. If you know people to have rust on their plants, ban them from your greenhouse. The same disease infests the rose bay willowherb, a plant which is related to the fuchsia, so these weeds should not be allowed to grow nearby. There is no method of biological control, so infected leaves must be picked off, placed in a sealed bag, and consigned to the trash can. Then spray all plants with a fungicide containing mancozeb.

Gray Mold, Botrytis (*Botrytis cinerea*)
This is the gray, rather woolly looking mold that attacks all decaying plant material. It needs cool, damp, still air to thrive, and is most commonly seen in the autumn and winter. Infected leaves and dead material must be removed immediately, and as much ventilation as possible supplied on suitable days. Electric heaters, with their drying effect, and circulating fans are helpful in controlling the disease. There are chemical methods to control botrytis, but if the damp, still conditions persist, the disease will return almost immediately.

Gray mold is one of the commonest diseases to affect plants growing in moist and cool conditions

73

Plant Directory

The descriptions and flower colors mentioned in this chapter are typical of each cultivar growing under average conditions in northwest Europe. Flower colors in particular can vary depending on growing and feeding methods, so these descriptions are only an approximate guide. As a general rule the more light the plants are given, the deeper the colors. The raiser's name, country of origin, and date of introduction, where known, are also given as an aid to identification, as there are many duplications of names (and

sometimes plants are known under different names in different countries). Where references are made to weeping standards, they refer to the method of growing plants over inverted hanging baskets or similar supports.

Special Note

There are two fuchsia hybridizers in Great Britain named David Clark, one being the author of this book. The fuchsias raised by the author are credited to D.W.H. Clark and the others to D. Clark.

Alf Thornley
D. Clark, Britain, 1981

Double. The pink tubes are short and the recurving sepals pink, tipped green. The beautifully shaped corolla is creamy white. The medium-sized blooms are formed on bushy, upright growth. This culti-var makes a perfect bush for decoration or exhibi-tion.

"Applause" is a fine cultivar with much appeal. It is slightly more delicate than some fuch-sias but it is worth taking the extra effort to grow it well

Anita
Raiser and date of introduction unknown

Single. The tube and sepals are white, and the corolla bright orange. The habit is strong and upright, but it needs pinching to keep it bushy. The small to medium-sized flowers are very freely produced and are held semi-erect. Do not confuse this cultivar with "Anita" raised by Niederholzer in 1946, which has double blooms.

Annabel
Ryle, Britain, 1977

Double. The large blooms are nearly pure white, and are only tinged with pink when grown in full sun. The growth is upright, and strong enough to support the massed weight of the flowers. The leaves are nor-mally pale green, but will change to a darker shade if overfed with a high nitro-gen fertilizer. This is a good general-purpose cul-tivar that can be grown as a bush, basket, or standard.

Army Nurse
Hodges, U.S.A., 1947

Semi-double. The blooms are medium-sized and have a red tube and sepals, with a bluish-purple corolla flushed and veined pink. Very hardy, and when planted in the garden makes a large, attractive bush. Good for planting in the center of a large decorative urn or pot.

Baby Bright
Bright, 1992

Single. The recurving sepals are white on top and pink underneath. The corolla is pale pink, almost white, with pink veining. The blooms appear in profusion on this bushy upright plant, which is usually taller than broad.

Applause
Stubbs, U.S.A., 1978

Double. The short tube and sepals are pale pink and the large corolla is pinkish-orange. The stems are short but strong. This beautiful cultivar is similar to "Marcus Graham" and was raised by the same grower. Best in pots or hanging baskets, but with care it can make an attractive standard.

arborescens

This is a species from Central America, particularly parts of Mexico and Guatemala. The tiny, lilac-colored blooms are borne in sprays that more resemble a lilac (*Syringa* sp.) than a fuchsia. The leaves

"Army Nurse" is an excellent garden shrub that can grow to a meter or more in height and spread, even in a frosty area. It can also be used to plant a low but dense hedge

are large, and growth strong. Although it will start flowering in a small pot, given time it will become a small tree. In southern Mexico it attains a height of 25-30 ft. (7.5-9 m). Alternative names for this species are *F. arborea, F. hamellioides,* and *F. ingaeflora.* See also the similar species *F. paniculata.*

Bicentennial
Paskesen, U.S.A., 1976

Double. The large blooms are freely produced. The tube and sepals are pale orange, and the corolla is orange on the outside and purple within. The growth is horizontal or trailing. Some growers find this cultivar difficult, but it can be trained as a good hanging basket or weeping standard.

Bland's New Striped
Bland, Britain, 1872

Single. This old cultivar has stood the test of time. The tube and recurving sepals are red, and the corolla is bright purple with pink streaks down the center of each petal. The blooms are large, and the habit is bushy and upright.

Beacon Rosa
Burgi-Ott, Switzerland, 1972

Single. The medium-sized blooms are freely formed on stiff, upright stems. The plant needs little training to form an attractive bush. It is a mutation from the red-and-purple "Beacon" which is very hardy. This sport, however, is not quite so vigorous and needs a sheltered spot outside to thrive.

Bealings
Goulding, Britain, 1983

Double. The medium to large blooms have a white tube and sepals, and a broad blue corolla. The color changes little with age and the habit is bushy and upright. An outstanding introduction of exceptional quality. Grow as a bush or standard.

Blush O'Dawn
Martin, U.S.A., 1962

Double. The very large blooms have a white tube and sepals, and a pale, silvery, gray-blue corolla. The stems are rather short and trail under the weight of the flowers. A rather slow-growing cultivar, but many consider it the best of its color. Best grown in a hanging pot or small basket.

boliviana var. luxurians alba

A variety of a species from Bolivia. Single. The long tube is white and up to 2-2 ½ in. (5-6 cm) long. The sepals and corolla are deep flame-red. Provide winter warmth and, as it grows quite large, a roomy greenhouse. The type species is similar but has a red tube instead of white and, like several of its varieties, has now naturalized in many countries. Crimson berries form after the flowers, adding to its beauty.

Opposite top: "Bealings." This is one of the best cultivars to be raised by Edwin Goulding at his nursery in Suffolk, England. The beautiful blooms are very striking and the plant becomes a firm favorite with everyone who grows it

Opposite bottom: "Beacon Rosa" is a sport from "Beacon." As it is not completely hardy it needs a sheltered place in the garden to survive

Left: "Bland's New Striped" is a very old British cultivar that is now grown mainly as a curiosity

Right: "Border Queen." As its name implies, this cultivar is particularly good in the garden border in summer

Border Queen
Ryle, Britain, 1974

Single. The sepals are white with a pink flush and green tips. The corolla is deep purplish-blue suffused with pink, particularly towards the base of the petals. The habit is upright and self-branching. This is a sister seedling to "Eden Lady" which is similar in appearance, but with slightly darker blooms.

Bountiful
Munkner, U.S.A., 1963

Double. The full and rounded corolla is white with pink veining. The tube and sepals are pale pink and tipped with green. The medium-sized blooms are continuously formed in great profusion. This cultivar is best grown in a basket but can be grown as a bush if well supported with canes.

Brutus
Lemoine, France, 1897

Single. Fuchsias as old as this, and still commonly grown, must have something special. The medium-sized red-and-purple blooms are freely produced on bushy, slightly limp stems. It can be grown easily into a bush, basket, standard, or any other form you wish. Hardy, it makes a nice garden shrub.

Caledonia
Lemoine, France, 1899

Single. The red tube is exceptionally long, the sepals are also red, and the corolla a slightly deeper crimson. Almost a self. In gardening a "self" is a bloom containing only one color. This cultivar is very hardy and is ideal for growing as a low hedge.

Bow Bells
Handley, British, 1972

Single or semi-double. The white tube is short and the long white sepals are tipped with green. The corolla is magenta with white at the base of the petals. The flowers are large and freely produced on long, rather limp stems. It can be grown as a bush but is better in a basket or trained as a standard.

Brookwood Belle
Gilbert, Britain, 1988

Double. So often the despairing cry is heard, "Oh no, not another red and white fuchsia." However, this is one of the best. The habit is upright, bushy and strong. The medium-sized red-and-white blooms appear in great profusion. An excellent large bush or standard.

Cardinal Farges
Rawlins, Britain, 1958

Semi-double. The medium-sized blooms have a shiny red tube and sepals and a white corolla veined with red. The habit is upright and it makes a superb free-flowering potted plant or is hardy in a sheltered garden. This plant is a sport from "Abbé Farges."

Carla Johnston
Pacey, Britain, 1986

Single. The tube and sepals are greenish-white, flushed red. The corolla is palest lavender, just off-white. The blooms face outward or slightly upward, and are freely produced on stiff, upright stems. Best grown as a bush, but it makes a nice standard with careful training.

Opposite top: "Brookwood Belle"

Opposite bottom: "Brutus"

Right: "Carla Johnson"

Below: "Caroline"

Caroline
Miller, Britain, 1967

Single. This beautiful cultivar is a seedling from "Citation," and has inherited its parent's wide-open or flaring corolla. The tube and sepals are pale pink, and the corolla is pale pinkish-lilac. The large, freely produced blooms form on upright stems. Difficult to train as a standard, it is best grown as a bush.

Cascade
Lagen, U.S.A., 1937

Single. The tube and long, thin sepals are pink and the corolla is deep red. The blooms appear in great profusion on bushy but very limp stems. This cultivar is very suitable for growing in a hanging basket or as a weeping standard.

81

Celia Smedley
Roe, Britain, 1970

Single. This is an extremely vigorous cultivar that will grow into a very large bush in the first season. The blooms are medium-sized with a pale red tube and sepals, and a bright red corolla. The stems are very strong and upright, with pale green leaves. This cultivar needs drastic pruning when being repotted in the spring or it will become very bare and woody at the base. It is also hardier than many realize and will survive outdoors in a sheltered position.

This outstanding cultivar was named after George Roe's daughter and is one of more than a dozen hybrids raised by him between 1970-1984. This plant was produced from a cross between "Joy Patmore" and "Glitters." Other fine introductions by this raiser include "Micky Goult," "Nellie Nuttall," and "Lady Thumb," all of which have won many prizes at shows.

Checkerboard
Walker and Jones, U.S.A., 1948

Single. The tube is red, the sepals white, and the corolla is deep red. The color changes are abrupt and striking. The growth is very strong and upright, and the blooms are freely produced. The plant is rather open in appearance so you can see all parts at the same time. With suitable training it will make a good bush and an excellent standard.

Opposite: "Celia Smedley"

Above: "Checker-board"

Above right: "Chillerton Beauty"

Chillerton Beauty
Bass, Britain, 1847

Single. The tube becomes pink on the side that faces the sun, and is cream on the shady side. The pink sepals open flat or recurve only slightly. The medium to small blooms have a blue corolla that fades to purplish-red. Growth is very strong and upright, so plant in the garden where it is very hardy. It is also known as "Query.". This presumably occurred when someone who did not know the correct name, wrote "Query" on the label.

China Lantern
Raiser and date of introduction unknown

Single. The glossy, deep-pink tube contrasts with the green tipped, white sepals. The corolla is pink with a white blotch at the base of the petals. The growth is rather limp but upright, and the medium-sized flowers are freely formed. Best as a potted plant, but suitable for hanging baskets or standards.

Citation
Hodges, U.S.A., 1953

Single. The large blooms have a pink tube and sepals, and a white corolla. The petals flare outward, creating a saucer shape. The blooms are freely produced, and the habit is upright and bushy. Not always the easiest plant to grow, it can be temperamental if the growing conditions are not to its liking. Best grown as a bush; standards can be difficult.

Cliff's Unique
Gadsby, Britain, 1976

Double. The white sepals are flushed with pink, and the corolla is pale blue. The medium-sized blooms are formed in exceptional profusion, even on small plants, and are held semi-erect. Growth is strong and bushy. Best grown as a bush, it will make a small standard with perseverance.

"Citation" is beautiful, but unless it is given ideal conditions, especially in winter, it can be rather temperamental

Constellation
Schnabel, U.S.A., 1957

Double. The medium to large blooms are white with a slight tendency to turn pink. The plant is vigorous and free-flowering and makes a good bush, standard, or pillar. Very attractive, it has only a slight greenness to the sepals, making it almost pure white.

Coquet Dale
Ryle, Britain, 1976

Double. The tube is short and very pale pink. The wide and flaring sepals are pale pink and the corolla is lilac. Some of the medium sized blooms have a few lilac petaloids. The growth is bushy, stiff, and upright. Very suitable for growing as a bush or standard.

Left.: "Devonshire Dumpling." The perfect fuchsia may never be raised, but this one comes very near with superb habit of growth and Immense production of flowers

Right: "Elise Mitchell" did not make an immediate impact when it was first introduced, but its fine qualities are now much appreciated

Drama Girl
Lockerble, Australia, 1975

Double. The tube and sepals are pale pink, and the corolla is bright blue with pink marbling. The habit is vigorous and bushy. It seems to know how to make a good hanging basket without being shown, and needs little training to make a good weeping standard.

Elise Mitchell
Ryle, Britain, 1980

Double. The medium-sized blooms are very freely formed on limp but upright growth. The tube and sepals are pale pink, and the corolla is pinkish-lavender, with a few splashes of pink. The plants are naturally bushy and need little training to bring them to their highest potential. Grow in a hanging basket or as a small standard.

Enchanted
Tiret, U.S.A., 1951

Double. A first-class cultivar that, excluding the bush form, can be trained into most shapes. The tube and sepals are red, and the corolla is deep blue overlaid with pink. The stems are long and trailing.

Left: "Estelle-Marie." This is one of a group of hybrids raised from "Bon Accorde" (called "Erecta Novelty" in the U.S.A.) which have flowers that are held outward or upward

Estelle-Marie
Newton, U.S.A., 1973

Single. The short tube is greenish-white and the sepals are white, tipped green. The corolla is mauve-violet with white at the base of each petal. The flowers are held semi-erect and appear on strong, thick, upright stems. Almost certainly a seedling from "Bon Accorde," which also hold its blooms erect. Best trained as a bush.

Flash
Hazard & Hazard, U.S.A., c. 1930

Single. The small blooms have a red tube, and a magenta corolla that fades to red. The plant is hardy and vigorous, and the stems are strong, upright, and moderately bushy. Its best feature is the color; uniform red being unusual, particularly in a hardy cultivar. It flowers fairly freely but starts rather late in the season. Can be grown in a greenhouse but it is happier outside.

Flowerdream
Rijff, Netherlands, 1983

Double. The short tube is pink and the sepals are white, with a pink patch near the tube on the upper side. The white corolla is formed as two layers – a tightly packed center, and a flaring outer layer. Growth is bushy and of moderate vigor, but the blooms are produced in great abundance. Can be grown as a bush, standard or hanging basket.

Above: fulgens is a large-growing but very attractive species that is best grown in large pots or directly in the greenhouse border

Opposite: "Flash." This cultivar is one of the most hardy red-flowered hybrids, although the tube and sepals are paler than the corolla

Fuchsiade 88
De Graaff, Netherlands, 1988

Single. The small to medium-sized blooms have a dusky red tube and sepals, and an intense beet-red corolla. The color can be almost black when newly opened. The flowers are freely formed on long, stiff stems. This unusual cultivar is proving to be very frost-resistant and comes into flower early when planted outdoors as a garden shrub. The same raiser has produced other cultivars such as "Haute Cuisine," "Gerharda's Aubergine," and "Mood Indigo," which have similar flower colors.

fulgens

A species from Mexico with varieties in Guatemala. The pale red tube is long, and the sepals are yellowish to green with a red base. The corolla is bright red. The blooms are very attractive and appear in clusters from the tips of the branches. The large, hairy leaves grow up to 9 in. (23 cm) long, and the roots are thick and partly tuberous. In the wild it forms a small shrub up to 48 in. (122 cm) high. Best grown in large pots or in a warm greenhouse border.

Glazioviana
Berry, U.S.A.

Single. This unusual and charming species was found by Dr. Paul Berry, from the Missouri Botanical Gardens, in the 1980s in the Cloud Forest around the Nova Friburgo, in South America. It was a natural shrubby growth and in its habitat can grow up to 13 ft. (4 m). The single flowers have a deep pink tube and petals. The corolla is purple. The foliage has a distinctive glossy sheen. It is short-jointed.

Golden Anniversary
Stubbs, U.S.A., 1981

Double. The very large blooms have a pure-white tube and sepals, and a very deep-blue corolla splashed with pink. The flowers appear very freely on long arching stems. This is another top-notch cultivar raised by Annabelle Stubbs. Best grown in a hanging basket or as a standard.

Garden News
Handley, Britain, 1978

Double. Being reliably hardy and having large flowers, it joins an elite group of double-flowered hardy cultivars such as "Prosperity" and "Lena" (but flowers slightly earlier). The short tube and sepals are pink, and the corolla magenta. The beautiful blooms come early and continue until the frost. Suitable for growing as a potted plant.

Garden Week
Richardson, Australia, 1985

Double. The tube and sepals are pale pink, and the corolla is mixed shades of cerise and deep orange. Growth is very strong and upright, but the size of the giant blooms weighs it down. Not exactly free-flowering, but if the production of blooms is limited by removing some of the buds, the remaining flowers can be large enough to cover your hand. Best grown as a hanging basket; it also makes a rather open standard.

Above: "Garden News." This is certainly one of the best double-flowered cultivars for planting permanently in the garden and was named after the British gardening newspaper

Right: Discovered by an American in South America, "Glazioviana" is a highly unusual fuchsia

Hampshire Blue
D.W.H. Clark, Britain, 1983

Single or semi-double. The medium-sized blooms have a white tube and sepals, and a pale, icy-blue corolla. Growth is upright and fairly free branching. Normally grown as a bush, it also makes a good standard. A sport from "Carmel Blue."

Hampshire Leonora
D.W.H. Clark, Britain, 1991

91

Double. This double sport from the single flowered "Leonora" is otherwise identical to its progenitor. The medium to large flowers are very freely formed on stiff, free-branching stems. The tube is cream and the sepals are pink, tinged cream, with green tips. The corolla is pale pink with a broad, lilac-pink patch at the base of each petal. Excellent as a bush or standard.

Above: "Hampshire Leonora." This double-flowered cultivar, raised by the author, is a sport from the single flowered "Leonora" raised by Horace Tiret in San Francisco (1964)

Left: "Greenpeace" is outstanding because of its greenish-yellow color. It is tall-growing and rather rampant, which may account for its surprising lack of popularity

Greenpeace
De Graaff, Netherlands, 1981

Single. A large, unusual cultivar. The tube and sepals are greenish-yellow, and the corolla is a paler shade of the same color; almost white. Growth is vigorous, tall, and fairly bushy. The blooms are very freely produced and it is best grown in a large pot or the greenhouse border. Best left unpruned as it dislikes being controlled.

Hampshire Treasure
D.W.H. Clark, Britain, 1983

Double. The tube and sepals are salmon-pink, and the corolla orange and cerise. Free flowering, even in winter, to the point where it is difficult to take cuttings. Growth is stiff but arching, so it can be grown in a pot, basket, or as a small standard.

Happy Wedding Day
Richardson, Australia, 1985

Double. The blooms are basically white, but faintly tinged with pink. The very strong stems tend to grow long and arch gracefully towards the horizontal. Best grown in large pots or hanging baskets. Though the blooms are large they are not really produced in sufficient numbers.

Harry Gray
Dunnett, Britain, 1981

Double. The white blooms are of medium size and often tinged with pink. Growth is very dense and bushy but can be almost hidden by the profusion of flowers. Small plants can be grown in pots but best grown in hanging baskets, despite the stems being limp rather than trailing.

Hawkshead
Travis, Britain, 1962

Single. The small white flowers have a slight greenish tinge and show little tendency to turn pink. Similar to *F. magellanica* var. *molinae* which is one of its parents, but is bushier and flowers more freely. Dislikes being grown under glass, but fortunately is hardy and makes a superb garden shrub.

Heidi Ann
Smith, Britain, 1969

Double. The habit is naturally very bushy, dense, and self-branching. It hardly needs any training to grow into a perfect bush. The tube and sepals are crimson, and the corolla is lilac. The medium-sized blooms appear in profusion. "Heidi Ann" is hardy, and can be used as a low-growing shrub at the front of a garden border.

"Heidi Ann." This cultivar and its sport, "White Heidi Ann," make wonderful potted plants as well as small shrubs in the garden

Hidcote Beauty
Webb, Britain, 1949

Single. There are so many cultivars that look the same or very similar that growers are always on the look out for a distinctly different color. This is it! The tube and sepals are creamy white, and the corolla a glorious salmon-pink. The actual shade is impossible to describe and photographs do not catch its subtlety; has to be seen to be appreciated. The quite large leaves are soft green with a slightly frosty look, and growth is strong. Although it is reasonably free-branching it responds well to pinching. Since growth arches gracefully it can be trained as a limp bush, hanging basket, or standard. Has the vigor to be trained as a pillar.

Hobson's Choice
Hobson, Britain, 1976

Double. The growth is very bushy, and the upright stems are strong and support the weight of the large flowers very well. The tube and sepals are deep pink, and the corolla is pale powder-pink. One of the best of the red-and-pink blooming cultivars. An excellent bush or standard.

Jeane
(syn. Genie, Genii)
Reiter, U.S.A., 1951

Single. The abundant blooms are cerise and deep violet, but they are more than rivaled by the beautiful lemon-yellow foliage. Extremely hardy, it makes a magnificent garden shrub or low hedge where the intensity of its leaf color has great impact. Growth is densely bushy and upright; for best effect, place in full sun. In Britain it is usually cataloged as "Genii" (Reiter). Mr. Reiter has confirmed that he did not raise such a cultivar, but his "Jeane" matches the description perfectly. It is assumed that the British name is a phonetic misspelling.

Hula Girl
Paskesen, U.S.A., 1972

Double. Similar to "Swingtime" but the blooms and stems grow larger. The giant flowers have a red tube and sepals, and a creamy-white corolla. Considering the size of the blooms they appear in great profusion. Best grown in large hanging baskets or as a weeping standard.

Right: "Jeane." The bright, lemon-yellow-colored foliage is one of the most attractive features of this very hardy cultivar

Below: "Hula Girl" is one of the best subjects for growing in a large hanging basket or training as a weeping standard

Jennie Rachel
Cheetham, Britain, 1979

Double. The tube is white, and the white sepals are slightly tinged pink, and tipped green. The corolla is rose-red and has petaloids of a similar shade. The strong, upright stems support the very large blooms. The leaves are also large and can grow up to 5 in. (13 cm) in long.

Kegworth Carnival
Smith, Britain, 1978

Single. The medium-sized blooms have a tube and sepals of glistening ice-white, and the corolla is a glowing shade of cerise. Naturally bushy but rather drooping, it is a colorful choice for a medium-sized hanging basket or standard. It is similar to the double-flowered "Duchess of Albany" which is thought superior by some.

Knockout
Stubbs, U.S.A., 1981

Double. The tube and sepals are pale salmon-pink. The corolla is striped with deep orange and purple. The stems are strong and want to grow upright, but arch horizontally under the weight of the flowers. Although the blooms are undoubtedly beautiful, the cultivar is intolerant of heat and has an unfortunate tendency to drop its leaves in mid-summer.

Koralle
Bonstedt, Germany, 1905

Single. Another member of the triphylla group, so named because the members look similar to *F. triphylla* from which they derive. The blooms are long and tapering, and are a one-tone, salmon-orange. The large leaves are bronze-green and are produced on long stems. The name of this cultivar is sometimes spelled "Coralle."

La Campanella
Blackwell, Britain, 1968

Semi-double. The tube and sepals are white, and the corolla is purple fading to lavender. The blooms are medium-sized but appear in great profusion. Growth is naturally short-jointed and bushy so it hardly needs any training, but the occasional pinch makes it even more impressive. The habit is fairly limp; while it can be grown in pots it is best in a hanging basket. This hybrid is another fine example that was found as a chance seedling rather than being the result of a deliberate cross.

Lady Isobel Barnett
Gadsby, Britain, 1968

Single. The tube and sepals are red, and the petals have broad, pale-mauve edges with a large central patch of near-white. The medium-sized blooms appear in great abundance and hold themselves out, but not quite upward. The stems are bushy, thick, and strong. Best grown as a bush.

Lady Thumb
Roe, Britain, 1966

Semi-double. A sport from "Tom Thumb." The blooms have a white corolla veined red; otherwise it is identical with its progenitor. See "Tom Thumb."

Laura
Raiser and date of introduction unknown

Single. The tube and sepals are pale orange, and the corolla is dusky orange. The medium-sized blooms are freely formed on a bushy, upright plant. It makes a good bush or standard. The name "Laura" has been used for at least three completely different cultivars: by Youell, in Britain, 1846; Nieder-holzer, U.S.A., 1946; and Martin, U.S.A., 1968.

Opposite: The beauty of "Kegworth Carnival" lies in the wonderful contrast between the ice-white tube and sepals and the deep cerise corolla

Right: "La Campanella" is one of the best subjects for a hanging basket, but although it is naturally bushy it responds well to extra pinching in the early stages of training

Lena
Bunney, Britain, 1862

Semi-double or double. With others such as "Marinka" and "Cascade," it is one of the classic plants for a hanging basket. The tube and sepals are white or pale pink, and the corolla is blue-purple with pink splashes. Growth is bushy and trailing, and the blooms appear in very great profusion. "Lena" is quite hardy (it also tolerates dry conditions) and makes a low, spreading shrub in the garden. Has one of the largest blooms for a hardy fuchsia. "Eva Boerg" seems to be a renaming of this wonderful old cultivar.

Leverhulme
Rehnelt, Germany, 1928

Single. A triphylla hybrid whose flowers are rather fatter and shorter than usual. The light-red blooms are also formed in smaller bunches than normal, and the leaves are smaller and have green instead of the more typical red undersides. Growth is upright; makes a colorful potted plant. Is sometimes cataloged as "Leverkusen."

Linda Goulding
Goulding, Britain, 1981

Single. The medium-sized blooms are white with a pink flush to the underside of the sepals. The habit is strong and bushy, and the stems grow stiff and upright. The flowers appear in great abundance, and tend to hold themselves out instead of hanging down. Grow as a bush or small standard.

"Marcus Graham." Since being shown on a national TV program, this fuchsia has become one of the most sought-after in Great Britain

Lord Lonsdale
Raiser and date of introduction unknown

Single. This cultivar has large leaves that are curled at the edges. When young the curling is more severe, producing a rolled and distorted leaf which may look diseased. This unfortunate tendency becomes less pronounced with maturity, and as growth slows down. The tube and sepals are pale orange, and the corolla is a superb tangerine-orange. The beautiful blooms are freely produced, but in the early stages the stems need frequent pinching to promote bushiness. Growth is strong and upright. Best cultivated as a bush. A hybrid with similar-colored flowers is "Clair de Lune." Its leaves are much larger than those of "Lord Lonsdale" and do not curl, but the blooms are not quite as abundant. "Aurora Superba," with light-orange flowers, is another beautiful plant which may be confused with "Lord Lonsdale."

Louise Emershaw
Tiret, U.S.A., 1972

Double. The thin tube and long sepals are white. The corolla, on opening, is rhodamine-purple but quickly changes to cerise-red. Growth is bushy, free-flowering and trailing. Best grown in a hanging basket or as a weeping standard.

magellanica "Aurea"

A variety of a species from Argentina and Chile. Single. A hardy variety with beautiful, deep golden-yellow foliage. The small red-and-purple blooms in late summer and autumn are a bonus. A vigorous plant making a hardy garden shrub or hedge. It does not grow quite as large as the green-leafed varieties of *F. magellanica*.

magellanica macrostemma "Versicolor"

A variety of a species from South America. Single. The foliage is silver-green with a red flush. The small, abundant flowers are usually red-and-purple, but red-and-mauve variants occur. Extremely hardy, it makes a very beautiful hedge or individual garden shrub.

Malibu Mist
Stubbs, U.S.A., 1985

Double. The large blooms have a bluish-violet corolla with a white center. The short tube and sepals are white, tinged with pink. The corolla changes color markedly with age, fading to purple. The growth is rather drooping but still stiff; makes a good hanging basket or bush.

Mancunian
Goulding, Britain, 1985

Double. The tube is pink and the sepals are white, tinged pink. The large corolla is white, with a pale pink flush and pink veining. Growth is strong and trailing. It looks magnificent as a hanging basket or weeping standard.

Above: "Margaret Brown" is a superb garden plant, either grown as a single specimen or as a hedge

Left: "Margaret Tebbit." The soft pastel colors are a main feature of this cultivar and the blooms look particularly attractive against the deep green foliage

Marcus Graham
Stubbs, U.S.A., 1985

Double. A beautiful cultivar with a white tube, and sepals that are sometimes tinged pink. The American raiser describes the corolla as pink striped with pale orange, but in Britain the color ranges from pale pink in winter, to pale apricot-orange in summer. The flowers are large, and the plant is bushy and upright. Train as a bush or standard.

Margaret
Wood, Britain, c. 1940

Semi-double. The tube and sepals are scarlet and the corolla is violet with paler petal bases. The medium-sized blooms appear very freely on bushy stems. This is a very hardy and vigorous cultivar that can grow up to 4 ft. (125 cm) in height and makes a fine hedge.

Margaret Brown
Wood, Britain, 1949

Single. The plant is very vigorous and it produces masses of small flowers that are virtually one tone, pale pink. Very hardy, it is best planted in the garden as it needs space to grow to its full potential. Also forms a dense, low hedge up to 36 in. (91 cm) high.

Margaret Tebbit
Dyos, 1992

Double. The tube is greenish-white, and the sepals are pale pink and recurve to touch each other. The corolla is white and the abundant, medium-sized blooms are especially attractive and freely produced. Growth is limp, but it can be trained as a bush; also looks good in a hanging basket.

Margaret Roe
Gadsby, Britain, 1968

Single. The medium-sized blooms appear very freely and are held outward or upright. The tube and sepals are red and the corolla is violet-purple. The habit is upright and bushy and it makes a good summer bedding plant.

Marilyn Olsen
Wilkinson, Britain, 1987

Single. The plant is small, upright and exceedingly bushy. The blooms have a pink tube and sepals, and a white corolla. The flowers may be small, but very freely appear. An outstanding exhibition bush, also good for general decoration.

Above: "Marilyn Olsen." This cultivar is one of the best exhibition quality fuchsias to be raised in recent years. The flowers are small but appear in great profusion

Right: "Marin Glow" is well named because the color of the corolla seems to glow and always attracts attention

of the classic plants for a hanging basket, some find it a little somber. Its variegated sport, "Golden Marinka," has light green-and-yellow leaves with identical flowers.

Although this cultivar has a brighter look than its progenitor, it grows much more slowly and flowers later. Like many variegated fuchsias it is slightly more tender and needs a warm greenhouse to survive winter. In Australia "Marinka" is also known as "Blaze.". Highly recommended for hanging baskets.

Marin Glow
Reedstrom, U.S.A., 1954

Single. The tube and sepals are white, and the medium-sized corolla is a shade of iridescent purple which only slightly changes color with age. The strong growth is upright and naturally bushy. Equally suitable for growing as a bush or standard.

Marinka
Rozain-Boucharlat, France, 1902

Single. The tube and sepals are red, and the corolla is a deeper shade of red. The flowers are only medium-sized but appear in very great profusion. Growth is vigorous and naturally trailing, with dark green leaves. Generally regarded as one

Above: "Marinka." Although it was raised almost one hundred years ago, this is one of the mostly widely cultivated fuchsias in hanging baskets. The only problem with this cultivar is that it tends to produce all its flowers at the ends of the longest stems, leaving the top rather bare

Mary
Bonstedt, Germany, 1894

Single. This beautiful cultivar is a member of the triphylla group and is said to be a cross between *F. triphylla* and *F. corymbiflora*. The 3 in.- (7.5 cm-) long blooms are one tone, bright scarlet, and appear in bunches. The leaves are large and deep-green with purple-red undersides. Best grown in pots or a warm greenhouse border.

Mayblossom
Pacey, Britain, 1984

Double. Growth is short-jointed and bushy, and as the stems are thin it trails. The abundant small flowers have a pink tube and sepals, and a white corolla. Ideal for growing in small pots or hanging baskets.

Micky Goult
Roe, Britain, 1981

Single. The white tube is short, and the sepals are white but pale-pink underneath. The small flowers have purple corollas and are held semi-erect. The mass of blooms form in clusters and the habit is upright, bushy, and compact. Ideal for exhibition as a bush.

microphylla

A species from Mexico. A member of the *encliandra* section of the genus *Fuchsia*. The flowers are tiny, measuring about ¼ in. (6 mm) long. The leaves are dark green, about ½ in. (13 mm) long, and give the plant a fern-like appearance. The tube and sepals are red and the corolla pink. This species is quite vigorous, and can be grown in a pot or planted permanently in the garden where it will thrive in a sheltered position.

Mieke Meursing
Hopwood, Britain, 1968

Single or semi-double. Originally named "Mrs. Mieke Meursing" after a president of the Netherlands Fuchsia Society, this wonderful cultivar was a chance seedling found growing under a plant of "R.A.F." The profusion of medium-sized blooms have a red tube and sepals, and a pink corolla. Growth is semi-upright and exceptionally bushy and short-jointed. Is easily formed into a specimen of exhibition quality with very little help from the grower. Also sold under the name "Pink Spangles."

Minirose
De Graaff, Netherlands, 1983

Single. The tube and sepals are a very pale rose, and the corolla is deep pink. The small blooms appear in profusion on upright, bushy stems. Is most suitable for pots, but may make a standard.

Miss California
Hodges, U.S.A., 1950

Semi-double. The tube and sepals are pink, the corolla white with a hint of pink, and the medium-sized flowers are very elegant and freely produced. The plant is rather slow to grow in the early stages, but is very rewarding in the long term. It normally grows upright and has easily trained growth. The habit is well-branched with semi-trailing stems. This cultivar must be shaded from direct sunlight as the leaves scorch very easily.

Below left: "Mieke Meursing." This excellent cultivar is equally suitable for general decoration or exhibiting. It can also be found under the name "Pink Spangles" in some non-specialty nurseries

Opposite: "Mary" has the typical long flowers of the triphylla group to which it belongs. To thrive it needs a large pot or to be planted in the greenhouse border

Moonraker
Clitheroe, Britain, 1979

Double. The tube and sepals are white, flushed pink. The sepals have green tips. The corollas are pale blue, with pale blue petaloids. The long flowers appear freely on strong, upright, bushy growth. May be trained as a bush or standard.

Morning Light
Waltz, U.S.A., 1960

Double. The tube and base of the sepals are red, and the rest of the sepals are white. The large corolla is bluish-lavender, splashed pink. The leaves are lemon-yellow but turn pale green if overfed. Growth is well-branched with semi-trailing stems. This delightful cultivar burns easily and is best grown in light shade. Can be trained as a bush, standard, or in a hanging basket.

Mr. A. Huggett
Raiser and date of introduction unknown

Single. The short tube and sepals are red, and the corolla is mauve-pink. The small to medium-sized blooms are produced on low, short-jointed stems. An excellent potted plant of show quality, it is also very hardy, and makes a nice shrub for the front of the garden border.

Mrs. Popple
Elliott, Britain, 1899

Single. This is one of the hardiest fuchsias, with the added bonus of having medium-sized flowers. The leaves are dark green, and the stems sturdy and bushy. The blooms have a red tube and sepals, and the corolla is darkest purple. Always one of the first hardy fuchsias to flower in the garden, it continues until stopped by frost. It also makes an excellent hedge.

"Mrs Popple." This old cultivar is one of the very best for permanently planting in the garden, either as an individual specimen or as a hedge

Neapolitan
D. Clark, Britain, 1984

Single. The flowers, although slightly larger than usual for a member of the *encliandra* section, are still very small. The blooms appear in three different colors at the same time – red, pink, and white. This may be due to instability in the plant's genetic makeup; it is certainly most unusual. Growth is strong and spreading. Suitable for growing in pots, it may also be trained into miniature standards, fans, espaliers, etc. See also *F. microphylla*.

Nicki's Findling
Ermel, 1985

Single. The tube and sepals are shades of orange, and the corolla is bright orange. The medium-sized blooms curve out and slightly upward. The habit is upright, bushy, and short-jointed. This beautiful cultivar can be grown as a bush or standard.

Above:
The freely produced blooms of "Orange Drops" have bright orange corollas, making it one of the best in this color range for baskets and standards

Left:
"Pacquesa" is a cultivar that is characterized by medium-sized, bright and shiny blooms that appear on stiff, upright stems

Orange Drops
Martin, U.S.A., 1967

Single. The perfect orange cultivar has not yet been raised, but this is better than most. The medium-sized blooms, which are freely produced, have a pale orange tube and sepals, and a bright orange corolla. It is reasonably self-branching but it needs frequent pinching to keep it tidy. Can be trained as a bush, hanging basket, or standard. Like most fuchsias with this flower color it is slightly more tender than usual. "Coachman" is a similar cultivar worth considering for hanging baskets.

Pacquesa
Clyne, Britain, 1974

Single. The medium-to large-sized blooms have a red tube and sepals, and a white corolla with red veining. The flowers very freely appear on stiff, upright stems. Growth is strong and fairly free-branching, but it responds well to pinching. Makes an ideal bush specimen.

Fuchsia paniculata is so unusual than many people do not realize that it is a fuchsia

paniculata

A species found from southern Mexico to Panama. This species is difficult to distinguish from *F. arborescens*. The main difference is that the sprays of flowers (panicles) are more open and purplish than the blooms of *arborescens*. The leaves are large and shaped like laurel.

Peachey
Stubbs, U.S.A., 1992

Double. The flowers are very large and attractive. The tube and sepals are white, and the corolla is a peachy orange-pink. With "Applause" and "Marcus Graham" it is another stunning cultivar raised by Annabelle Stubbs in the U.S.A.

Peppermint Stick
Walker and Jones, U.S.A., 1950

Double. If I were asked to nominate one cultivar as the best all-around fuchsia, this is it. "Peppermint Stick" makes a superb bush, pillar, pyramid, or standard of any size. It also fills a large hanging basket but does not produce long, trailing stems. It seems to have a joy of life that even an inexperienced grower finds difficult to curb, for it looks green, vigorous and healthy even when it has no right to do so. The abundant large blooms have a red tube and sepals, and the full corolla is purple, boldly striped in rose.

Pinch Me
Tiret, U.S.A., 1969

Double. The stems are stiff but arch down in flower. The medium to large blooms have a white tube and sepals, and a rich blue corolla. The name is rather misleading as it needs little pinching to make a magnificent hanging basket. Rather sensitive to direct sunlight, it can easily burn if not shaded.

Pink Fantasia
Webb, Britain, 1989

Single. The medium-sized flowers have a pink tube and sepals, and a purplish corolla. Naturally very bushy, the plant is vigorous and upright, and will grow large quite quickly. Just a few pinches will bring it to full show standard. "Rose Fantasia" is a sport that is similar, but the corolla is rosy-mauve.

Pink Galore
Fuchsia-La Nurseries, U.S.A., 1958

Double. As its name implies, it produces masses of large, one-tone, pink blooms. The trailing stems grow very long, and need frequent pinching to make them bushy. The flowers are only produced at the extreme ends of the branches, so keep growing by appropriate feeding or it will flower in flushes. Only suitable for growing in hanging baskets or as a weeping standard.

Pink Marshmallow
Stubbs, U.S.A., 1971

Double. The gigantic white flowers are very freely produced on long, trailing stems. Makes a superb hanging basket, and needs a larger-than-average container to reach its full potential. The leaves are pale green and endure sun quite well, although the blooms will then become tinged with pink. Young plants can look a little disappointing, rather like spaghetti with leaves! This is normal and will not affect the delights to come.

Right: "Peppermint Stick" is an easy-to-grow fuchsia that can be trained into almost any shape. Beginners and experts alike love this cultivar

Opposite bottom: "Pink Fantasia." This cultivar, and its sport "Rose Fantasia" are very popular as show plants as they are very free flowering and exceptionally easy to train into a bush

Above: "Piper" has one of the largest blooms for a hardy fuchsia and is also unusual (for a hardy cultivar) in having near-white flowers

Above right: "Pink Marshmallow" is best grown in a hanging basket where its giant blooms can be seen to their greatest advantage

Pinto
Walker and Jones, U.S.A., 1956

Double. The huge blooms are very freely produced on naturally trailing growth. The tube and sepals are light red, and the corolla is white splashed with deep pink. An eye-catching cultivar, it is suitable for a hanging basket or as a weeping standard.

Piper
Howarth, Britain, 1985

Double. The large blooms are white with a pink flush. Growth is vigorous and upright. The raiser has tested this cultivar for several years in an open garden in Wales. If long-term trials confirm its hardiness, it will be by far the largest white-flowered, hardy fuchsia available, and so far looks very promising. A cross between "White Ensign" and "White Spider."

Left: "Preston Guild." This stunning hardy plant has blooms that fade from bright blue to cerise

President Margaret Slater
Taylor, Britain, 1972

Single. The tube is white and the long, twisted sepals are white flushed with pink, tipped green. The corolla is mauve-pink with a salmon flush. The medium-sized flowers appear very freely on a bushy, naturally trailing plant. Excellent for hanging baskets and standards, and a great favorite with exhibitors.

Preston Guild
Thornley, Britain, 1971

Single. The long tube and sepals are glistening white. The corolla, as it opens, is deep sky-blue but fades to cerise. The old and new flower colors are very distinct, suggesting the plant has two different types of bloom. Growth is strong and uncompromisingly upright. Reasonably hardy, it makes a large shrub in a mild area.

procumbens

A species native to New Zealand. This species has tiny blooms that are remarkable because the tube is yellow, the sepals are green and purple, the filaments red-orange, and the anthers are covered with blue pollen; it does not have a corolla. The flowers point upward and are followed by large, plum-colored fruits. The plant has long, thin, trailing stems that creep along the ground. Hardy in the garden, but the drainage must be good; rockeries are ideal. Must be grown in the sun or it will grow luxuriantly at the expense of flowers.

Prosperity
Gadsby, Britain, 1970

Double. This cultivar benefits from two main qualities — it is reliably hardy, and has large double flowers. Only a few plants such as "Garden News" and "Lena" share these attributes. The tube and sepals are red and shiny, and the corolla is white with noticeable red veining. The stems are thick, strong, and upright. Although very valuable in the garden, it can also be grown in pots.

Quasar
Walker, U.S.A., 1974

Double. The very large blooms are very freely produced on limp stems. While it can be grown as a potted plant, it is best in hanging baskets. The tube and sepals are white, and the corolla pale blue. "Stanley Cash" is similar, but has a deeper-blue corolla.

Queen of Derby
Gadsby, Britain, 1975

Double. The tube and sepals are red, and the corolla is deep blue with pink stripes. The leaves are deep green and clothe the strong, upright stems. Good for training as a potted plant, it is also reliably hardy in a sheltered spot in the garden.

R.A.F.
Garson, U.S.A., 1942

Double. Considering they are large, the blooms are borne in great profusion. The tube and sepals are red, and the corolla is dusky pink. The habit is drooping. Can be grown in a pot, hanging basket, or as a standard. "Fascination" has similar flowers, but this hybrid is temperamental and is not so easy to cultivate.

Rose of Castile Improved
Banks, Britain, 1869

Single. The author is unhappy with this name. It is not like "Rose of Castile," and it certainly is not an improvement, except that it is much hardier in the open garden. The tube and sepals are light red, and the corolla is bluish-purple. The medium-sized blooms are larger than "Rose of Castile" but less abundant, and the growth is stronger and taller. Best in the open garden, or in pots trained as a bush.

Rose of Denmark
Banks, Britain, 1864

Single. The medium-sized blooms are nearly one shade of mid-pink. The stems are strong, numerous and bushy, and trail gracefully downward. The blooms are very freely produced. One of the easiest cultivars to grow in a hanging basket, it also makes a superb weeping standard.

Royal Velvet
Waltz, U.S.A., 1962

Double. An excellent potted plant or standard. The very large blooms have the classic shape with a red tube and sepals, and a glorious purple corolla. Growth is strong and semi-upright. "Voo-Doo" is somewhat similar but has larger blooms, and the corolla is a rather dull, reddish-purple.

Riccartonii
Young, Britain, c. 1830

Single. The tube and sepals are bright red, and the corolla deep purple. The blooms are medium-sized and freely produced. Growth is very strong and upright, and it is extremely hardy. Can be seen naturalized in many parts of Ireland and southwest England. A good hedging plant, it can reach 4 ft. 6 in. (1.4 m) high. It hates cultivation under glass; the slightest hot, dry spell makes the leaves drop.

Rose of Castile
Banks, Britain, 1855

Single. This old cultivar is still commonly grown for a very good reason. It produces masses of medium-sized blooms on an easy growing, bushy plant, with stiff upright stems. The tube and sepals are white, and the purplish-blue corollas have a whitish patch at the bases of the petals. Makes a good potted plant or standard, and is hardy in a sheltered spot in the garden.

Above: "R.A.F." This cultivar, named in the U.S.A. during the Second World War, makes a wonderful hanging basket. The same raiser also produced "Winston Churchill" (1942)

Right: "Royal Velvet." If you want to grow a bush fuchsia with very large red-and-purple blooms, then this is the cultivar to grow

Roy Walker
Walker, U.S.A., 1975

Double. The medium-sized, rather globular blooms are almost pure white, having just a faint pink flush. The abundant flowers appear on ultra-compact, short-jointed growth which, when small, does not need any support. Flowers rather late in the season, well after most other cultivars. Best grown as a bush trained potted plant, and kept in a warm greenhouse through the winter.

Rufus
Nelson, U.S.A., 1952

Single. The blooms are nearly one shade of light red. A very vigorous culti-var, it should be kept well-pinched. Makes a large bush and can be grown into a large standard quite quickly. Also worth trying as a hardy shrub, but it needs a sheltered position. It is also incorrectly known as "Rufus the Red."

Ruth King
Tiret, U.S.A., 1967

Double. The short tube and sepals are red, and the full corollas are striped with pastel shades of lilac, pink, and white. The blooms are large and borne on long, arching stems, so it can be trained as a bush, standard, or grown in hanging baskets.

Santa Cruz
Tiret, U.S.A., 1947

Double. The medium-sized blooms are virtually one shade of dark crim-son. Growth is very strong and upright. Makes a splendid garden shrub, but can be grown in pots if it is pinched frequently while young.

Seventh Heaven
Stubbs, U.S.A., 1981

Double. The very large blooms have a white tube and sepals, and a red corolla with just a hint of orange. Growth is very strong and stiff and, though starting upright, it arches down with age. A very beautiful and differ-ent cultivar, but perhaps the blooms could appear just a little more freely. Best grown in a large pot, hanging basket, or as a standard.

Opposite: "Silver Breckland" is a beautiful sport which was first noticed by Jill Clark, the author's wife, growing on a plant of "Breckland" in 1992, and was released for sale in 1995

Left: "Santa Cruz." The most hardy fuchsias tend to have small flowers, so the medium-sized, bright red blooms of this culti-var are a sen-sation in the garden

Sharpitor
National Trust, Britain, 1974

Single. A very hardy shrub that dislikes potted plant culture under glass; plant outdoors once it has filled a 4 in. (10 cm) or larger pot with roots. The small leaves are pale green and yellow, and the small, not very freely pro-duced blooms are pale pink. Growth is quite strong and the plants are very bushy. Good in the garden for its unusual leaf color.

Silver Breckland
D.W.H. Clark, Britain, 1995

Single. A sport from "Breckland." The white tube is very short, and the sepals pink, brightening towards the base of the tube. The corolla is sil-very-lavender and opens wide, but not quite flat. The leaves are dark green, and the habit is upright and bushy. Looks best when trained as a bush.

Snowfire
Stubbs, U.S.A., 1978

Double. The flowers are large and basically white, but the corolla is boldly striped with deep pink. The stems are strong and arch down to the horizontal. The habit is greatly improved with a few early pinches. Suitable for pots, hanging baskets, and standards.

Sophisticated Lady
Martin, U.S.A., 1964

Double. The shape of the flower buds is long and tapering. The blooms have a pale pink tube and sepals, and creamy-white corollas. Responds well to pinching, and forms masses of trailing stems that have all the substance of wet string. Being incredibly free flowering it makes a superb basket or weeping standard. Do not try to train as a conventional standard because the stems are not stiff enough.

Above: "Space Shuttle." The wonderful flowers are particularly valued because the corolla is deep creamy-yellow

Right: "Sparky," with its distinctive coloring, is a fuchsia that is hard to ignore

South Gate
Walker and Jones, U.S.A., 1951

Double. Easily grown, it has large, very pretty blooms in a shade of pale pink; the sepals are green tipped. The stems are strong but arch over, so it can be grown in a pot or hanging basket; easily makes a standard.

Space Shuttle
De Graaff, Netherlands, 1981

Single. The long flowers have a red tube, and the sepals are green with red at the base. The corolla is also red at the base, changing to yellow. The leaves are very large and slightly hairy with an unpleasant smell. The abundant blooms appear on stems that need the support of canes. A highly unusual hybrid, it becomes quite large and is best for large pots or the greenhouse border.

Sparky
Webb, Britain, 1994

Single. Unusual triphylla-type fuchsia. The flowers are all purple and are held semi-erect, standing out from the stem. The foliage is a distinctive dark bronze. "Sparky" is a slow grower, but the unusual coloring of both flowers and foliage makes it a fuchsia that is hard to ignore. It can be used ideally as an "accent plant" in containers, but is not hardy.

Left: "Stella Ann" is a member of the triphylla group with salmon-orange blooms

Below: "String of Pearls" is aptly named, as the blooms are formed in a string along each stem

Squadron Leader
Goulding, Britain, 1986

Double. The exquisite medium to large blooms are white, but have a pale pink blush on the corollas. The drooping growth branches well, and is able to support the masses of flowers. Fine in a hanging basket.

Stanley Cash
Pennisi, U.S.A., 1970

Double. The very large blooms have a white tube, and sepals with deep blue corollas. Attractive and free-flowering, it initially grows upright but trails down under the weight of the blooms. See "Quasar."

Stella Ann
Baker-Dunnett, Britain, 1974

Single. A member of the triphylla group. The abundant blooms are in several shades of salmon-orange. The broad leaves are dark bronzy-green with red undersides. The habit is strong, upright and bushy.

String of Pearls
Pacey, Britain, 1976

Single to semi-double. The tube and sepals are very pale pink, and the corolla is pale lavender. The stems are long and arching, and the medium-sized flowers are carried in a line towards the tip. Needs pinching as it is not naturally bushy, but is attractive and well worth cultivating. Grow as a standard or bush.

Sugar Almond
Hobson, Britain, 1978

Double. The medium-sized blooms are palest pink and the habit is bushy, stiff and upright. A good cultivar for planting in the center of an urn or a mixed hanging basket where the upright nature is required.

Swingtime
Tiret, U.S.A., 1950

Double. The blooms are large, verging on very large. The tube and sepals are bright red, and the full and wide corolla is white with a few red veins. Growth is vigorous, and the strong stems have just the right amount of substance to arch gracefully under the great weight of flowers. Makes a superb hanging basket or standard.

Opposite: "Thalia" is the most commonly grown member of the triphylla group of fuchsias. Although it is rather more tender than most, it revels in outdoor conditions in the summer

Above: "Swingtime" is an outstanding cultivar that is perfect for growing in a hanging basket or as a standard

Taffeta Bow
Stubbs, U.S.A., 1974

Double. Another fine introduction from Annabelle Stubbs. The very large blooms are long rather than wide, and have deep pink sepals that curl like a bow. The corollas are violet-purple. The stems are very strong and trailing. Can be grown in a hanging basket or makes a large weeping standard.

Tennessee Waltz
Walker and Jones, U.S.A., 1951

Double. The tube and sepals are pink, and the corolla is lavender-blue, splashed with pink. The large blooms freely appear on upright, bushy stems. Hardy, it received a Highly Commended award for hardiness in the Royal Horticultural Society trials, 1962-1978. It also makes an excellent potted plant, basket, or standard.

Texas Longhorn
Fuchsia-La Nurseries, U.S.A., 1960

Semi-double. This cultivar became very famous because it gained the reputation of having the largest fuchsia blooms. Certainly the red sepals are very long and can reach 9 in. (23 cm) from tip to tip. The white corolla is relatively small, however, and the flowers lack substance and are not freely formed. Growth is willowy and does not respond very well to training. I mention it here in the hope that you will *not* waste your time growing it. Probably only listed by nurseries because some growers still demand it.

Thalia
Bonstedt, Germany, 1905

Probably the most popular member of the triphylla group. The long, tapering red blooms appear at the ends of the stems. Growth is strong and upright, and the large leaves are dark green with a red reverse. Similar to "Gartenmeister Bonstedt," which only differs in having a slightly more bulbous tube.

The Aristocrat
Waltz, U.S.A., 1953

Double. The long tube is creamy white, and the sepals are pink-tipped white. The corolla is white with pink veins. The outer petals are also tinged with pale pink. The large, full blooms are very appealing and freely form on upright, bushy stems.

Tom Thumb
Baudinat, France, 1850

Single or semi-double. The tube and sepals are carmine, and the corolla purple. The blooms are small but appear in great profusion. Growth is upright and extremely bushy. Under glass it can be grown in small pots and needs a pinch or two when young. Outdoors it is very hardy and forms low, dense mounds and makes an ideal rockery

Left: "Torville and Dean." This fine cultivar is named after the British Olympic gold medal-winning ice-skaters

Right: "Waldfee" has tiny blooms that are typical of the section of the genus to which it belongs. Although small, the flowers are freely produced

plant. The sports "Lady Thumb" and "Son of Thumb" are equally hardy, and have white and lavender corollas respectively. The latter appears to have occurred before, being named "Mrs. Ida Noach" by the French grower Lemoine in 1911.

Tom West
Meillez, France, 1853

Single. The small red-and-purple blooms appear very late in the season. It is grown purely for the attractive, red-suffused, green-and-cream foliage. The habit is limp, so it can be grown in a pot or hanging basket. Exhibits a fair degree of hardiness and is worth trying in a sheltered garden border.

Torville and Dean
Pacey, Britain, 1985

Double. The large blooms have a pink tube and sepals, and a white corolla delicately flushed with pink. Growth is upright, short-jointed, and bushy. Best grown as a bush in pots. The blooms are almost identical to "Cotton Candy."

Trail Blazer
Reiter, U.S.A., 1951

Double. The large flowers have a long corolla and are a shade of cerise red. The blooms freely appear on very drooping stems. Makes an excellent hanging basket or weeping standard.

Waveney Gem
Burns, Britain, 1985

Single. This is a gem; magnificent for the show-bench. The blooms are small to medium-sized and have a white tube and sepals, and a pink corolla with a flush of lavender. The naturally very bushy growth is rather drooping so it spreads out horizontally rather than upwards. Can be grown in a pot, but is best suited to a hanging basket or even makes a standard.

Waveney Waltz
Burns, Britain, 1982

Single. The abundant, medium-sized blooms appear on upright, bushy growth, similar to "Flirtation Waltz" which is one of its parents. The tube and sepals are pale pink, and the corolla is white. Makes a good bush or standard.

Venus Victrix
Gulliver, Britain, 1840

Single. This chance seeding is the first recorded cultivar with a white tube and it is thought that all white-tubed hybrids have this plant as an ancestor. The blooms are small but have attractive bright-blue corollas. The growth is rather weak and straggly. Interesting rather than useful. It is said to have been sold for the equivalent of $1.60 when first released to the public in 1842.

Waldfee
Travis, Britain, 1973

Single. This is a typical member of the *encliandra* section of the genus Fuchsia. The tiny flowers are about ½ in. (1 cm) long and are soft lilac-pink. The growth is strong, upright, and hardy except in the coldest areas. It can be trained as a bush, small standard, or even as a bonsai.

"Waveney Waltz." The pink-and-white blooms are the most striking feature of this excellent cultivar

Right: "Waveney Gem." The dense, dark-green foliage makes a perfect foil for the flowers

Wave of Life
Henderson, Britain, 1869

Single. The small flowers are scarlet and purple. The main beauty of this cultivar is in the golden-yellow leaves with pinkish-red stems. The habit is fairly dense and bushy, and it makes a very unusual hanging basket or standard.

White Heidi Ann

Double. A sport from "Heidi Ann," with the same bushy, self-branching habit as its progenitor, but the blooms have a white corolla instead of mauve. The sport has occurred several times and can be found listed as "Heidi Weiss" and "White Ann."

Right: "Wicked Queen." The blooms are large and, although it was released as hardy, I would only recommend planting it permanently in a sheltered position

Below: "White Heidi Ann" is a white sport from the lavender "Heidi Ann." Like its progenitor, it makes a good bush or low garden shrub

White Pixie
Merrist-Wood College, Britain, 1968

Single. This is a sport of "Pixie" that has occurred many times, probably even earlier than the date given. The tube and sepals are red and the corolla white with red veins. The leaves are greenish-yellow and the medium-sized blooms appear freely. The growth is bushy, upright, and very hardy.

Whiteknights Pearl
Wright, Britain, 1980

Single. The long tube and sepals are cream, and often tinged with pink. The corolla is a nice pale pink. The medium to small blooms are produced on very vigorous upright growth with slightly saw-edged leaves. The habit is upright and bushy and, as it is very hardy, it makes a good garden specimen. It also grows well in the greenhouse provided it is planted in a large pot or the border.

Wicked Queen
Tabraham, Britain, 1985

Double. The tube and sepals are red, and the corolla is deep blue, splashed with pink. The flowers are large and freely produced. An excellent potted plant cultivar, it is hardy in a sheltered spot in the garden.

Right: "Whiteknights Pearl" makes a large garden shrub and its pale pink flowers, although not large, are very freely produced

Left: "White Pixie." This cultivar and "Jeane" are two very hardy cultivars with attractive yellow foliage

Winston Churchill
Garson, U.S.A., 1942

Double. The tube and sepals are red, and the short but full corolla is light blue. The medium-sized flowers are generously produced on short-jointed, upright stems. "Rose Churchill" is a sport with a deep pink corolla, the other characteristics being identical. Both cultivars are best grown in pots and bush-trained. They deteriorate rather badly in winter and need higher temperatures than average to survive.

Recommended Species and Cultivars

The following is by no means a complete list. It is just a selection of those cultivars and species mentioned in the Plant Directory that are the easiest to grow. Those recommended for growing as standards are also suitable for growing as pillars, fans, espaliers, and pyramids.

For Growing as a Bush

"Bealings"

"Brookwood Belle"

"Brutus"

"Carla Johnston"

"Celia Smedley"

"Checkerboard"

"Devonshire Dumpling"

"Hampshire Leonora"

"Heidi Ann"

"Hobson's Choice"

"Marilyn Olsen"

"Marin Glow"

"Mieke Meursing"

"Minirose"

"Pacquesa"

"Peppermint Stick"

"Rose of Castile"

"Royal Velvet"

"Tennessee Waltz"

For Growing in Hanging Baskets

"Cascade"

"Dancing Flame"

"Deep Purple"

"Drama Girl"

"Elise Mitchell"

"Harry Gray"

"Hula Girl"

"La Campanella"

"Lena"

"Mancunian"

"Marinka"

"Orange Drops"

"Pinch Me"

"Pink Marshmallow"

"Quasar"

"Rose of Denmark"

"Sophisticated Lady"

"Squadron Leader"

"Swingtime"

"Waveney Gem"

For Growing as Conventional Standards

"Annabel"

"Brookwood Belle"

"Brutus"

"Checkerboard"

"Constellation"

"Devonshire Dumpling"

"Hampshire Leonora"

"Peppermint Stick"

"Rose of Castile"

"Royal Velvet"

"Rufus"

"Southgate"

"Tennessee Waltz"

For Growing as Weeping Standards

(These must be trained over an inverted hanging basket or similar support.)

"Enchanted"

"Golden Anniversary"

"Hula Girl"

"Lena"

"Mancunian"

"Marinka"

"Pink Marshmallow"

"Rose of Denmark"

"Swingtime"

Hardy Shrubs For Permanent Garden Planting

(The figures quoted show the average height reached in trials in southern England. They will vary greatly from place to place, depending on the severity of winters and the amount of shelter given to the plants.)

	Height
"Army Nurse"	41 in. (104 cm)
"Brutus"	26 in. (66 cm)
"Chillerton Beauty"	26 in. (66 cm)
"Fuchsiade 88"	24 in. (61 cm)
"Garden News"	24 in. (61 cm)
"Hawkshead"	30 in. (76 cm)
"Heidi Ann"	16 in. (41 cm)
"Jeane"	28 in. (71 cm)
"Lady Thumb"	16 in. (41 cm)
magellanica "Aurea"	31 in. (79 cm)
magellanica macrostemma "Versicolor"	35 in. (89 cm)
"Margaret"	48 in. (122 cm)
"Margaret Brown"	42 in. (107 cm)
"Mr. A. Huggett"	20 in. (51 cm)
"Mrs. Popple"	48 in. (122 cm)
"Piper"	24 in. (61 cm)
"Preston Guild"	20 in. (51 cm)
procumbens	5 in. (13 cm)
"Prosperity"	28 in. (71 cm)
"Riccartonii"	48 in. (122 cm)
"Tennessee Waltz"	26 in. (66 cm)
"Tom Thumb"	16 in. (41 cm)

Fuchsias Suitable For Hedges

	Height	Planting Distance
F. magellanica "Aurea"	31 in. (79 cm)	30 in. (6 cm)
magellanica macrostemma Versicolor	35 in. (89 cm)	30 in. (76 cm)
"Margaret"	48 in. (122 cm)	36 in. (91 cm)
"Margaret Brown"	42 in. (107 cm)	35 in. (89 cm)
"Mrs. Popple"	48 in. (122 cm)	30 in. (76 cm)
"Riccartonii"	48 in. (122 cm)	30 in. (76 cm)

Glossary, Bibliography and Index

Bibliography

American Fucshia Society Staff. *Checklist of Fuchsias Registered*, American Fuchsia Society, 1973 onwards

American Fucshia Society Staff. *Fuchsias Judging School Manual & A.F.S. Rules*, American Fuchsia Society, 1986

Bartlett, George. *The Complete Guide*, Crowood Gardening Press, 1994

Bartlett, George. *Fuchsias for House and Garden*, Crowood Gardening Press, 1994

Berry, P.E. The Systematic and Evolution of Fuchsia section *Fuchsia (Onagraceae) Annals of the Missouri Botanic Garden*. **69** (1) 209-234

Boullemier, L.B. *The Checklist of Species, Hybrids and Cultivars of the Genus Fuchsia*, Blandford Press, 1985

Boullemier, Leo. *A Plantsman's Guide to Fuchsias*, Ward Lock, 1989

Clapham, S. *Fuchsias for House and Garden*, David & Charles, 1982

Clark, D.W.H. *The Fuchsia Guide*, Oakleigh Publications, 1992

Clark, D.W.H. *Fuchsias for Greenhouse and Garden*, Collingridge, 1987

Clark, D.W.H. *The Hardy Fuchsia Guide*, Oakleigh Publications, 1990

Clark, Jill R. *Fuchsias*, Century Hutchinson, 1988

Ewart, R. *Fuchsia Lexicon*, 2nd. revised edition, Cassell, 1987

Goulding, Edwin. *Fuchsias, The Complete Guide*, Batsford, 1995

Munz, P.A. A Revision of the Genus *Fuchsia* (Onagraceae). *Proceedings of the California Academy of Natural Sciences*. **25** (I) I-138

Nijhuis, Miep. *500 More Fuchsias*, Batsford, 1996

Nijhuis, Miep (editor). *Fuchsias, The Complete Handbook*, Cassell, 1994

Nijhuis, Miep. *1000 Fuchsias*, Batsford, 1996

Proudley, B & V. *Fuchsias in Colour*, Blandford Press, 1975

Saunders, E. *Wagtail's Book of Fuchsias*, Wagtail's Publications Vol. 1-5 1987

Wilson, S.J. *Fuchsias*, Faber & Faber, 1974

Glossary

Anther
The tip of the stamen. The part of the flower that carries the pollen.

Berry
The fleshy fruit that follows the flower.

Break
To send out new growth. This can be the result of pinching out the growing tips or more drastic pruning.

Calyx
The part of the flower that consists of the sepals and tube.

Corolla
That part of the flower that consists of the petals.

Cultivar
Meaning a cultivated variety; a plant that has been deliberately bred or selected and is not found growing in the wild.

Dormancy
A temporary state of rest induced by low temperatures and dryness.

Filament
The stalk connected to an anther.

Genus
A group of species with common structural characteristics that are supposed to have derived from a common ancestor.

Hardy
Plants that can be permanently planted in the garden. The term is applied here to fuchsias that are being grown in countries where they are subjected to frost.

Hybrid
Botanically, a plant produced by crossing two species or sub-species. In common usage a plant that is not a species or variety of a species; synonymous with cultivar.

Internode
The length of stem between two pairs of leaves.

Leaf axil
The point on the stem where leaves join and new shoots emerge.

Leaf node
The swollen area where leaves join the main stem, including the leaf axil.

Ovary
The female portion of the flower that contains embryo seeds.

Petaloid
With fuchsias this refers to the small, short petals that occur in some blooms at the base of the corolla. Also refers to sepals and stamens that sometimes assume petal-like shapes.

Petiole
The leaf stalk.

Pinching out
The removal of the growing tip of a stem.

Pistil
The collective name for the ovary, style and stigma.

Pot back
The process of removing old soil from a plant's roots, and replanting it in a smaller container.

Pot on
To remove a plant from its pot and replant it, with minimum disturbance, in a larger container with fresh compost.

Repot
To remove old soil from the roots and replant with fresh compost in the same size pot.

Section
A group of very closely related plants contained within the genus.

Sepals
The outer parts of the flower bud that open to reveal the corolla.

Species
A group of botanically similar plants that are, or were, found in the wild and come true from seed.

Sport
A mutation that produces a flower or foliage variation in a cultivar or species.

Stamen
The filament and anther.

Stigma
The enlarged tip of the style that receives the pollen.

Stopping
Synonymous with pinching out.

Style
The stalk of the stigma that connects it to the ovary.

Tube
The narrow section of the flower that connects the ovary to the sepals and corolla.

Variety
A minor but distinct variation of a species but of insufficient importance to justify it as a separate species.

Index

ACKNOWLEDGMENTS

The publishers would like to thank David Clark at
Oakleigh Nurseries and Carol Gubler at Little Brook
Nurseries for their help in providing fuchsias
for photography

Artwork by Sara Philpot

PHOTOGRAPHIC ACKNOWLDGMENTS

David Clark 66, 67, 97 top, 114 bottom;

Hunt Institute for Botanical Documentation, Carnegie
Mellon University, Pittsburgh, PA, USA 14 left;

Image Select 14 right, /Ann Ronan Picture Library 13;

Oxford Scientific Films /J.A. L. Cooke 72;

Reed International Books Ltd. /Peter Myers endpapers,
1, 2 /3, 4 /5, 6 /7, 9, 10 /11, 11 , 15 , 16 , 17 , 17 , 18 /19,
19 inset, 21 , 23, 25, 28 , 29 bottom, 29 top, 30 , 32 top,
32 bottom, 34 bottom, 34 top, 36, 37, 38, 39, 40, 41,
42 /3, 45 bottom, 46, 47, 48, 52, 53 above center, 53 top,
53 below center, 53 bottom, 54 /5, 56 bottom left, 56 top,
56 bottom right, 57, 58 left, 59, 60 left, 60 right, 61, 63,
64, 68 /69, 69, 70, 71, 74 /5, 76, 77, 78 top, 78 bottom,
79 bottom, 79, 80 bottom, 80 top, 81 left, 81 right, 82,
83 left, 83 right, 84 left, 84 right, 85, 86 left, 86 right,
87 left, 87 right, 88 right, 88 left, 89, 92, 93 bottom,
93 top, 94, 95, 96, 97 bottom, 98 top, 98 bottom, 99,
100, 101, 102, 103 bottom, 103 top, 104 top, 104 bottom,
105 bottom, 105 top left, 105 top right, 106, 107 top,
107 bottom, 108, 109, 110 top, 110 bottom, 111 top,
111 bottom, 112, 113, 114 left, 115 bottom, 115 top,
116 top, 116 bottom, 117 top, 117 bottom, 118 /119, 119;

Science Photo Library /Dr Jeremy Burgess 73;

Simply Controls 44 left, 44 /5